THE POEMS

OF

ALGERNON CHARLES SWINBURNE

IN SIX VOLUMES

VOLUME III

POEMS AND BALLADS
SECOND AND THIRD SERIES
AND
SONGS OF THE SPRINGTIDES

LONDON
CHATTO & WINDUS
1912

Fifth Impression

CONTENTS

POEMS AND BALLADS

SECOND SERIES

	PAGE
THE LAST ORACLE	5
IN THE BAY	11
A FORSAKEN GARDEN	22
RELICS	26
AT A MONTH'S END	29
SESTINA	34
THE YEAR OF THE ROSE	36
A WASTED VIGIL	39
THE COMPLAINT OF LISA	42
FOR THE FEAST OF GIORDANO BRUNO	48
AVE ATQUE VALE	50
MEMORIAL VERSES ON THE DEATH OF THÉOPHILE GAUTIER	58
SONNET (WITH A COPY OF *MADEMOISELLE DE MAUPIN*)	66
AGE AND SONG (TO BARRY CORNWALL)	67
IN MEMORY OF BARRY CORNWALL	69
EPICEDE	72
TO VICTOR HUGO	74
INFERIAE	75
A BIRTH-SONG	77
EX-VOTO	81

	PAGE
A Ballad of Dreamland	85
Cyril Tourneur	87
A Ballad of François Villon	88
Pastiche	90
Before Sunset	92
Song	93
A Vision of Spring in Winter	94
Choriambics	98
At Parting	100
A Song in Season	101
Two Leaders	107
Victor Hugo in 1877	109
Child's Song	110
Triads	111
Four Songs of Four Seasons :—	
I. Winter in Northumberland	113
II. Spring in Tuscany	122
III. Summer in Auvergne	125
IV. Autumn in Cornwall	127
The White Czar	129
Rizpah	131
To Louis Kossuth	132
Translations from the French of Villon :—	
The Complaint of the Fair Armouress	133
A Double Ballad of Good Counsel	137
Fragment on Death	139
Ballad of the Lords of Old Time	140
Ballad of the Women of Paris	142
Ballad written for a Bridegroom	144

CONTENTS

PAGE

BALLAD AGAINST THE ENEMIES OF FRANCE . . 146

THE DISPUTE OF THE HEART AND BODY OF FRANÇOIS
VILLON 148

EPISTLE IN FORM OF A BALLAD TO HIS FRIENDS . 150

THE EPITAPH IN FORM OF A BALLAD . . . 152

FROM VICTOR HUGO 154

NOCTURNE 155

THÉOPHILE GAUTIER 157

ODE 158

IN OBITUM THEOPHILI POETÆ 160

AD CATULLUM 161

DEDICATION, 1878 162

POEMS AND BALLADS

THIRD SERIES

MARCH : AN ODE 169

THE COMMONWEAL 174

THE ARMADA 187

TO A SEAMEW 211

PAN AND THALASSIUS 215

A BALLAD OF BATH 222

IN A GARDEN 224

A RHYME 226

BABY-BIRD 228

OLIVE 230

A WORD WITH THE WIND 234

NEAP-TIDE 238

BY THE WAYSIDE 241

NIGHT 243

CONTENTS

	PAGE
IN TIME OF MOURNING	244
THE INTERPRETERS	245
THE RECALL	248
BY TWILIGHT	249
A BABY'S EPITAPH	250
ON THE DEATH OF SIR HENRY TAYLOR	251
IN MEMORY OF JOHN WILLIAM INCHBOLD	252
NEW YEAR'S DAY	257
TO SIR RICHARD F. BURTON	258
NELL GWYN	259
CALIBAN ON ARIEL	260
THE WEARY WEDDING	261
THE WINDS	270
A LYKE-WAKE SONG	271
A REIVER'S NECK-VERSE	272
THE WITCH-MOTHER	273
THE BRIDE'S TRAGEDY	276
A JACOBITE'S FAREWELL	281
A JACOBITE'S EXILE	282
THE TYNESIDE WIDOW	286
DEDICATION	289

SONGS OF THE SPRINGTIDES

TO EDWARD JOHN TRELAWNY	293
THALASSIUS	295
ON THE CLIFFS	311
THE GARDEN OF CYMODOCE	326
BIRTHDAY ODE	341
NOTES	359

POEMS AND BALLADS

SECOND SERIES

THE LAST ORACLE

(A.D. 361)

εἴπατε τῷ βασιλῆϊ, χαμαὶ πέσε δαίδαλος αὐλά·
οὐκέτι Φοῖβος ἔχει καλύβαν, οὐ μάντιδα δάφνην,
οὐ παγὰν λαλέουσαν · ἀπέσβετο καὶ λάλον ὕδωρ.

YEARS have risen and fallen in darkness or in twilight,
  Ages waxed and waned that knew not thee nor thine,
While the world sought light by night and sought
    not thy light,
  Since the sad last pilgrim left thy dark mid shrine.
Dark the shrine and dumb the fount of song thence
    welling,
  Save for words more sad than tears of blood, that
    said :
Tell the king, on earth has fallen the glorious dwelling,
  And the watersprings that spake are quenched and
    dead.
Not a cell is left the God, no roof, no cover
  In his hand the prophet laurel flowers no more.
And the great king's high sad heart, thy true last
    lover,
  Felt thine answer pierce and cleave it to the core.
    And he bowed down his hopeless head
      In the drift of the wild world's tide,
     And dying, *Thou hast conquered*, he said,
      Galilean ; he said it, and died.

And the world that was thine and was ours
When the Graces took hands with the Hours
Grew cold as a winter wave
In the wind from a wide-mouthed grave,
As a gulf wide open to swallow
   The light that the world held dear.
O father of all of us, Paian, Apollo,
   Destroyer and healer, hear !

Age on age thy mouth was mute, thy face was
   hidden,
   And the lips and eyes that loved thee blind and
     dumb ;
Song forsook their tongues that held thy name for-
   bidden,
   Light their eyes that saw the strange God's king-
     dom come.
Fire for light and hell for heaven and psalms for
   pæans
   Filled the clearest eyes and lips most sweet of song,
When for chant of Greeks the wail of Galileans
   Made the whole world moan with hymns of wrath
     and wrong.
Yea, not yet we see thee, father, as they saw thee,
   They that worshipped when the world was theirs
     and thine,
They whose words had power by thine own power
   to draw thee
   Down from heaven till earth seemed more than
     heaven divine.
     For the shades are about us that hover
      When darkness is half withdrawn
     And the skirts of the dead night cover
      The face of the live new dawn.

For the past is not utterly past
Though the word on its lips be the last,
And the time be gone by with its creed
When men were as beasts that bleed,
As sheep or as swine that wallow,
    In the shambles of faith and of fear.
O father of all of us, Paian, Apollo,
    Destroyer and healer, hear !

Yet it may be, lord and father, could we know it,
  We that love thee for our darkness shall have light
More than ever prophet hailed of old or poet
  Standing crowned and robed and sovereign in thy
    sight.
To the likeness of one God their dreams enthralled
    thee,
  Who wast greater than all Gods that waned and
    grew ;
Son of God the shining son of Time they called thee,
  Who wast older, O our father, than they knew.
For no thought of man made Gods to love or honour
  Ere the song within the silent soul began,
Nor might earth in dream or deed take heaven upon
    her
  Till the word was clothed with speech by lips of
    man.
    And the word and the life wast thou,
      The spirit of man and the breath ;
    And before thee the Gods that bow
      Take life at thine hands and death.
    For these are as ghosts that wane,
    That are gone in an age or twain ;
    Harsh, merciful, passionate, pure,
    They perish, but thou shalt endure ;

Be their flight with the swan or the swallow,
  They pass as the flight of a year.
O father of all of us, Paian, Apollo,
  Destroyer and healer, hear !

Thou the word, the light, the life, the breath, the
    glory,
  Strong to help and heal, to lighten and to slay,
Thine is all the song of man, the world's whole
    story ;
  Not of morning and of evening is thy day.
Old and younger Gods are buried or begotten
  From uprising to downsetting of thy sun,
Risen from eastward, fallen to westward and for-
    gotten,
  And their springs are many, but their end is one.
Divers births of godheads find one death appointed,
  As the soul whence each was born makes room for
    each ;
God by God goes out, discrowned and disanointed,
  But the soul stands fast that gave them shape and
    speech.
      Is the sun yet cast out of heaven ?
        Is the song yet cast out of man ?
      Life that had song for its leaven
        To quicken the blood that ran
      Through the veins of the songless years
      More bitter and cold than tears,
      Heaven that had thee for its one
      Light, life, word, witness, O sun,
      Are they soundless and sightless and hollow,
        Without eye, without speech, without ear ?
      O father of all of us, Paian, Apollo,
        Destroyer and healer, hear !

Time arose and smote thee silent at his warning,
  Change and darkness fell on men that fell from
      thee ;
Dark thou satest, veiled with light, behind the morn-
      ing,
  Till the soul of man should lift up eyes and see.
Till the blind mute soul get speech again and eye-
      sight,
  Man may worship not the light of life within ;
In his sight the stars whose fires grow dark in thy
      sight
  Shine as sunbeams on the night of death and sin.
Time again is risen with mightier word of warning,
  Change hath blown again a blast of louder
      breath ;
Clothed with clouds and stars and dreams that melt
      in morning,
  Lo, the Gods that ruled by grace of sin and death !
    They are conquered, they break, they are
        stricken,
      Whose might made the whole world pale ;
    They are dust that shall rise not or quicken
      Though the world for their death's sake wail.
    As a hound on a wild beast's trace,
    So time has their godhead in chase ;
    As wolves when the hunt makes head,
    They are scattered, they fly, they are fled ;
    They are fled beyond hail, beyond hollo,
      And the cry of the chase, and the cheer.
  O father of all of us, Paian, Apollo,
      Destroyer and healer, hear !

Day by day thy shadow shines in heaven beholden,
  Even the sun, the shining shadow of thy face :

King, the ways of heaven before thy feet grow
    golden ;
  God, the soul of earth is kindled with thy grace.
In thy lips the speech of man whence Gods were
    fashioned,
  In thy soul the thought that makes them and un-
    makes ;
By thy light and heat incarnate and impassioned,
  Soul to soul of man gives light for light and takes.
As they knew thy name of old time could we know it,
  Healer called of sickness, slayer invoked of wrong,
Light of eyes that saw thy light, God, king, priest,
    poet,
  Song should bring thee back to heal us with thy
    song.
      For thy kingdom is past not away,
        Nor thy power from the place thereof hurled ;
    Out of heaven they shall cast not the day,
      They shall cast not out song from the world.
    By the song and the light they give
    We know thy works that they live ;
    With the gift thou hast given us of speech
    We praise, we adore, we beseech,
    We arise at thy bidding and follow,
      We cry to thee, answer, appear,
  O father of all of us, Paian, Apollo,
      Destroyer and healer, hear !

IN THE BAY

I

Beyond the hollow sunset, ere a star
Take heart in heaven from eastward, while the west,
Fulfilled of watery resonance and rest,
Is as a port with clouds for harbour bar
To fold the fleet in of the winds from far
That stir no plume now of the bland sea's breast :

II

Above the soft sweep of the breathless bay
Southwestward, far past flight of night and day,
Lower than the sunken sunset sinks, and higher
Than dawn can freak the front of heaven with fire,
My thought with eyes and wings made wide makes
     way
To find the place of souls that I desire.

III

If any place for any soul there be,
Disrobed and disentrammelled ; if the might,
The fire and force that filled with ardent light
The souls whose shadow is half the light we see,
Survive and be suppressed not of the night ;
This hour should show what all day hid from me.

IV

Night knows not, neither is it shown to day,
By sunlight nor by starlight is it shown,
Nor to the full moon's eye nor footfall known,
Their world's untrodden and unkindled way.
Nor is the breath nor music of it blown
With sounds of winter or with winds of May.

V

But here, where light and darkness reconciled
Hold earth between them as a weanling child
Between the balanced hands of death and birth,
Even as they held the new-born shape of earth
When first life trembled in her limbs and smiled,
Here hope might think to find what hope were worth.

VI

Past Hades, past Elysium, past the long
Slow smooth strong lapse of Lethe—past the toil
Wherein all souls are taken as a spoil,
The Stygian web of waters—if your song
Be quenched not, O our brethren, but be strong
As ere ye too shook off our temporal coil;

VII

If yet these twain survive your worldly breath,
Joy trampling sorrow, life devouring death,
If perfect life possess your life all through
And like your words your souls be deathless too,
To-night, of all whom night encompasseth,
My soul would commune with one soul of you.

VIII

Above the sunset might I see thine eyes
That were above the sundawn in our skies,
Son of the songs of morning,—thine that were
First lights to lighten that rekindling air
Wherethrough men saw the front of England rise
And heard thine loudest of the lyre-notes there—

IX

If yet thy fire have not one spark the less,
O Titan, born of her a Titaness,
Across the sunrise and the sunset's mark
Send of thy lyre one sound, thy fire one spark,
To change this face of our unworthiness,
Across this hour dividing light from dark.

X

To change this face of our chill time, that hears
No song like thine of all that crowd its ears,
Of all its lights that lighten all day long
Sees none like thy most fleet and fiery sphere's
Outlightening Sirius—in its twilight throng
No thunder and no sunrise like thy song.

XI

Hath not the sea-wind swept the sea-line bare
To pave with stainless fire through stainless air
A passage for thine heavenlier feet to tread
Ungrieved of earthly floor-work? hath it spread
No covering splendid as the sun-god's hair
To veil or to reveal thy lordlier head?

XII

Hath not the sunset strewn across the sea
A way majestical enough for thee?
What hour save this should be thine hour—and mine,
If thou have care of any less divine
Than thine own soul; if thou take thought of me,
Marlowe, as all my soul takes thought of thine?

XIII

Before the moon's face as before the sun
The morning star and evening star are one
For all men's lands as England.   O, if night
Hang hard upon us,—ere our day take flight,
Shed thou some comfort from thy day long done
On us pale children of the latter light!

XIV

For surely, brother and master and lord and king,
Where'er thy footfall and thy face make spring
In all souls' eyes that meet thee wheresoe'er,
And have thy soul for sunshine and sweet air—
Some late love of thine old live land should cling,
Some living love of England, round thee there.

XV

Here from her shore across her sunniest sea
My soul makes question of the sun for thee,
And waves and beams make answer.   When thy feet
Made her ways flowerier and their flowers more
    sweet
With childlike passage of a god to be,
Like spray these waves cast off her foemen's fleet.

XVI

Like foam they flung it from her, and like weed
Its wrecks were washed from scornful shoal to shoal,
From rock to rock reverberate ; and the whole
Sea laughed and lightened with a deathless deed
That sowed our enemies in her field for seed
And made her shores fit harbourage for thy soul.

XVII

Then in her green south fields, a poor man's child,
Thou hadst thy short sweet fill of half-blown joy,
That ripens all of us for time to cloy
With full-blown pain and passion ; ere the wild
World caught thee by the fiery heart, and smiled
To make so swift end of the godlike boy.

XVIII

For thou, if ever godlike foot there trod
These fields of ours, wert surely like a god.
Who knows what splendour of strange dreams was
    shed
With sacred shadow and glimmer of gold and red
From hallowed windows, over stone and sod,
On thine unbowed bright insubmissive head ?

XIX

The shadow stayed not, but the splendour stays,
Our brother, till the last of English days.
No day nor night on English earth shall be
For ever, spring nor summer, Junes nor Mays,
But somewhat as a sound or gleam of thee
Shall come on us like morning from the sea.

XX

Like sunrise never wholly risen, nor yet
Quenched ; or like sunset never wholly set,
A light to lighten as from living eyes
The cold unlit close lids of one that lies
Dead, or a ray returned from death's far skies
To fire us living lest our lives forget.

XXI

For in that heaven what light of lights may be,
What splendour of what stars, what spheres of flame
Sounding, that none may number nor may name,
We know not, even thy brethren ; yea, not we
Whose eyes desire the light that lightened thee,
Whose ways and thine are one way and the same.

XXII

But if the riddles that in sleep we read,
And trust them not, be flattering truth indeed,
As he that rose our mightiest called them,—he,
Much higher than thou as thou much higher than
     we—
There, might we say, all flower of all our seed,
All singing souls are as one sounding sea.

XXIII

All those that here were of thy kind and kin,
Beside thee and below thee, full of love,
Full-souled for song,—and one alone above
Whose only light folds all your glories in—
With all birds' notes from nightingale to dove
Fill the world whither we too fain would win.

XXIV

The world that sees in heaven the sovereign light
Of sunlike Shakespeare, and the fiery night
Whose stars were watched of Webster ; and beneath,
The twin-souled brethren of the single wreath,
Grown in kings' gardens, plucked from pastoral heath,
Wrought with all flowers for all men's heart's delight.

XXV

And that fixed fervour, iron-red like Mars,
In the mid moving tide of tenderer stars,
That burned on loves and deeds the darkest done,
Athwart the incestuous prisoner's bride-house bars ;
And thine, most highest of all their fires but one,
Our morning star, sole risen before the sun.

XXVI

And one light risen since theirs to run such race
Thou hast seen, O Phosphor, from thy pride of place.
Thou hast seen Shelley, him that was to thee
As light to fire or dawn to lightning ; me,
Me likewise, O our brother, shalt thou see,
And I behold thee, face to glorious face ?

XXVII

You twain the same swift year of manhood swept
Down the steep darkness, and our father wept.
And from the gleam of Apollonian tears
A holier aureole rounds your memories, kept
Most fervent-fresh of all the singing spheres,
And April-coloured through all months and years.

XXVIII

You twain fate spared not half your fiery span ;
The longer date fulfils the lesser man.
Ye from beyond the dark dividing date
Stand smiling, crowned as gods with foot on fate.
For stronger was your blessing than his ban,
And earliest whom he struck, he struck too late.

XXIX

Yet love and loathing, faith and unfaith yet
Bind less to greater souls in unison,
And one desire that makes three spirits as one
Takes great and small as in one spiritual net
Woven out of hope toward what shall yet be done
Ere hate or love remember or forget.

XXX

Woven out of faith and hope and love too great
To bear the bonds of life and death and fate :
Woven out of love and hope and faith too dear
To take the print of doubt and change and fear :
And interwoven with lines of wrath and hate
Blood-red with soils of many a sanguine year.

XXXI

Who cannot hate, can love not ; if he grieve,
His tears are barren as the unfruitful rain
That rears no harvest from the green sea's plain,
And as thorns crackling this man's laugh is vain.
Nor can belief touch, kindle, smite, reprieve
His heart who has not heart to disbelieve.

XXXII

But you, most perfect in your hate and love,
Our great twin-spirited brethren ; you that stand
Head by head glittering, hand made fast in hand,
And underfoot the fang-drawn worm that strove
To wound you living ; from so far above,
Look love, not scorn, on ours that was your land.

XXXIII

For love we lack, and help and heat and light
To clothe us and to comfort us with might.
What help is ours to take or give ? but ye—
O, more than sunrise to the blind cold sea,
That wailed aloud with all her waves all night,
Much more, being much more glorious, should you be.

XXXIV

As fire to frost, as ease to toil, as dew
To flowerless fields, as sleep to slackening pain,
As hope to souls long weaned from hope again
Returning, or as blood revived anew
To dry-drawn limbs and every pulseless vein,
Even so toward us should no man be but you.

XXXV

One rose before the sunrise was, and one
Before the sunset, lovelier than the sun.
And now the heaven is dark and bright and loud
With wind and starry drift and moon and cloud,
And night's cry rings in straining sheet and shroud,
What help is ours if hope like yours be none?

C 2

A FORSAKEN GARDEN

In a coign of the cliff between lowland and highland,
  At the sea-down's edge between windward and lee,
Walled round with rocks as an inland island,
  The ghost of a garden fronts the sea.
A girdle of brushwood and thorn encloses
  The steep square slope of the blossomless bed
Where the weeds that grew green from the graves
    of its roses
      Now lie dead.

The fields fall southward, abrupt and broken,
  To the low last edge of the long lone land.
If a step should sound or a word be spoken,
  Would a ghost not rise at the strange guest's hand?
So long have the grey bare walks lain guestless,
  Through branches and briars if a man make way,
He shall find no life but the sea-wind's, restless
      Night and day.

The dense hard passage is blind and stifled
  That crawls by a track none turn to climb
To the strait waste place that the years have rifled
  Of all but the thorns that are touched not of time.
The thorns he spares when the rose is taken ;
  The rocks are left when he wastes the plain.
The wind that wanders, the weeds wind-shaken,
      These remain.

Not a flower to be pressed of the foot that falls not ;
  As the heart of a dead man the seed-plots are
    dry ;
From the thicket of thorns whence the nightingale
  calls not,
  Could she call, there were never a rose to reply.
Over the meadows that blossom and wither
  Rings but the note of a sea-bird's song ;
Only the sun and the rain come hither
    All year long.

The sun burns sere and the rain dishevels
  One gaunt bleak blossom of scentless breath.
Only the wind here hovers and revels
  In a round where life seems barren as death.
Here there was laughing of old, there was weeping,
  Haply, of lovers none ever will know,
Whose eyes went seaward a hundred sleeping
    Years ago.

Heart handfast in heart as they stood, "Look thither,"
  Did he whisper ? " look forth from the flowers to
    the sea ;
For the foam-flowers endure when the rose-blossoms
  wither,
  And men that love lightly may die—but we ? "
And the same wind sang and the same waves
  whitened,
  And or ever the garden's last petals were shed,
In the lips that had whispered, the eyes that had
  lightened,
    Love was dead.

Or they loved their life through, and then went
    whither ?
  And were one to the end—but what end who
    knows ?
Love deep as the sea as a rose must wither,
  As the rose-red seaweed that mocks the rose.
Shall the dead take thought for the dead to love
    them ?
  What love was ever as deep as a grave ?
They are loveless now as the grass above them
      Or the wave.

All are at one now, roses and lovers,
  Not known of the cliffs and the fields and the sea.
Not a breath of the time that has been hovers
  In the air now soft with a summer to be.
Not a breath shall there sweeten the seasons hereafter
  Of the flowers or the lovers that laugh now or
    weep,
When as they that are free now of weeping and
    laughter
      We shall sleep.

Here death may deal not again for ever ;
  Here change may come not till all change end.
From the graves they have made they shall rise up
    never,
  Who have left nought living to ravage and rend.
Earth, stones, and thorns of the wild ground growing,
  While the sun and the rain live, these shall be ;
Till a last wind's breath upon all these blowing
      Roll the sea.

Till the slow sea rise and the sheer cliff crumble,
 Till terrace and meadow the deep gulfs drink,
Till the strength of the waves of the high tides
  humble
 The fields that lessen, the rocks that shrink,
Here now in his triumph where all things falter,
 Stretched out on the spoils that his own hand
  spread,
As a god self-slain on his own strange altar,
  Death lies dead.

RELICS

THIS flower that smells of honey and the sea,
White laurustine, seems in my hand to be
   A white star made of memory long ago
Lit in the heaven of dear times dead to me.

A star out of the skies love used to know
Here held in hand, a stray left yet to show
   What flowers my heart was full of in the days
That are long since gone down dead memory's flow.

Dead memory that revives on doubtful ways,
Half hearkening what the buried season says
   Out of the world of the unapparent dead
Where the lost Aprils are, and the lost Mays.

Flower, once I knew thy star-white brethren bred
Nigh where the last of all the land made head
   Against the sea, a keen-faced promontory,
Flowers on salt wind and sprinkled sea-dews fed.

Their hearts were glad of the free place's glory ;
The wind that sang them all his stormy story
   Had talked all winter to the sleepless spray,
And as the sea's their hues were hard and hoary.

Like things born of the sea and the bright day,
They laughed out at the years that could not slay,
   Live sons and joyous of unquiet hours,
And stronger than all storms that range for prey.

And in the close indomitable flowers
A keen-edged odour of the sun and showers
   Was as the smell of the fresh honeycomb
Made sweet for mouths of none but paramours.

Out of the hard green wall of leaves that clomb
They showed like windfalls of the snow-soft foam,
   Or feathers from the weary south-wind's wing,
Fair as the spray that it came shoreward from.

And thou, as white, what word hast thou to bring?
If my heart hearken, whereof wilt thou sing?
   For some sign surely thou too hast to bear,
Some word far south was taught thee of the spring.

White like a white rose, not like these that were
Taught of the wind's mouth and the winter air,
   Poor tender thing of soft Italian bloom,
Where once thou grewest, what else for me grew
    there?

Born in what spring and on what city's tomb,
By whose hand wast thou reached, and plucked for
    whom?
   There hangs about thee, could the soul's sense tell,
An odour as of love and of love's doom.

Of days more sweet than thou wast sweet to smell,
Of flower-soft thoughts that came to flower and fell,
  Of loves that lived a lily's life and died,
Of dreams now dwelling where dead roses dwell.

O white birth of the golden mountain-side
That for the sun's love makes its bosom wide
  At sunrise, and with all its woods and flowers
Takes in the morning to its heart of pride !

Thou hast a word of that one land of ours,
And of the fair town called of the Fair Towers,
  A word for me of my San Gimignan,
A word of April's greenest-girdled hours.

Of the old breached walls whereon the wallflowers ran
Called of Saint Fina, breachless now of man,
  Though time with soft feet break them stone by
    stone,
Who breaks down hour by hour his own reign's span.

Of the old cliff overcome and overgrown
That all that flowerage clothed as flesh clothes bone,
  That garment of acacias made for May,
Whereof here lies one witness overblown.

The fair brave trees with all their flowers at play,
How king-like they stood up into the day !
  How sweet the day was with them, and the night !
Such words of message have dead flowers to say.

This that the winter and the wind made bright,
And this that lived upon Italian light,
  Before I throw them and these words away,
Who knows but I what memories too take flight ?

AT A MONTH'S END

THE night last night was strange and shaken :
  More strange the change of you and me.
Once more, for the old love's love forsaken,
  We went out once more toward the sea.

For the old love's love-sake dead and buried,
  One last time, one more and no more,
We watched the waves set in, the serried
  Spears of the tide storming the shore.

Hardly we saw the high moon hanging,
  Heard hardly through the windy night
Far waters ringing, low reefs clanging,
  Under wan skies and waste white light.

With chafe and change of surges chiming,
  The clashing channels rocked and rang
Large music, wave to wild wave timing,
  And all the choral water sang.

Faint lights fell this way, that way floated,
  Quick sparks of sea-fire keen like eyes
From the rolled surf that flashed, and noted
  Shores and faint cliffs and bays and skies.

The ghost of sea that shrank up sighing
  At the sand's edge, a short sad breath
Trembling to touch the goal, and dying
  With weak heart heaved up once in death—

The rustling sand and shingle shaken
  With light sweet touches and small sound—
These could not move us, could not waken
  Hearts to look forth, eyes to look round.

Silent we went an hour together,
  Under grey skies by waters white.
Our hearts were full of windy weather,
  Clouds and blown stars and broken light.

Full of cold clouds and moonbeams drifted
  And streaming storms and straying fires,
Our souls in us were stirred and shifted
  By doubts and dreams and foiled desires.

Across, aslant, a scudding sea-mew
  Swam, dipped, and dropped, and grazed the sea :
And one with me I could not dream you ;
  And one with you I could not be.

As the white wing the white wave's fringes
  Touched and slid over and flashed past—
As a pale cloud a pale flame tinges
  From the moon's lowest light and last—

As a star feels the sun and falters,
  Touched to death by diviner eyes—
As on the old gods' untended altars
  The old fire of withered worship dies—

(Once only, once the shrine relighted
   Sees the last fiery shadow shine,
Last shadow of flame and faith benighted,
   Sees falter and flutter and fail the shrine)

So once with fiery breath and flying
   Your winged heart touched mine and went,
And the swift spirits kissed, and sighing,
   Sundered and smiled and were content.

That only touch, that feeling only,
   Enough we found, we found too much ;
For the unlit shrine is hardly lonely
   As one the old fire forgets to touch.

Slight as the sea's sight of the sea-mew,
   Slight as the sun's sight of the star :
Enough to show one must not deem you
   For love's sake other than you are.

Who snares and tames with fear and danger
   A bright beast of a fiery kin,
Only to mar, only to change her
   Sleek supple soul and splendid skin ?

Easy with blows to mar and maim her,
   Easy with bonds to bind and bruise ;
What profit, if she yield her tamer
   The limbs to mar, the soul to lose ?

Best leave or take the perfect creature,
   Take all she is or leave complete ;
Transmute you will not form or feature,
   Change feet for wings or wings for feet.

Strange eyes, new limbs, can no man give her ;
  Sweet is the sweet thing as it is.
No soul she hath, we see, to outlive her ;
  Hath she for that no lips to kiss ?

So may one read his weird, and reason,
  And with vain drugs assuage no pain.
For each man in his loving season
  Fools and is fooled of these in vain.

Charms that allay not any longing,
  Spells that appease not any grief,
Time brings us all by handfuls, wronging
  All hurts with nothing of relief.

Ah, too soon shot, the fool's bolt misses !
  What help ? the world is full of loves ;
Night after night of running kisses,
  Chirp after chirp of changing doves.

Should Love disown or disesteem you
  For loving one man more or less ?
You could not tame your light white sea-mew,
  Nor I my sleek black pantheress.

For a new soul let whoso please pray,
  We are what life made us, and shall be.
For you the jungle and me the sea-spray,
  And south for you and north for me.

But this one broken foam-white feather
  I throw you off the hither wing,
Splashed stiff with sea-scurf and salt weather,
  This song for sleep to learn and sing—

Sing in your ear when, daytime over,
   You, couched at long length on hot sand
With some sleek sun-discoloured lover,
   Wince from his breath as from a brand :

Till the acrid hour aches out and ceases,
   And the sheathed eyeball sleepier swims,
The deep flank smoothes its dimpling creases,
   And passion loosens all the limbs :

Till dreams of sharp grey north-sea weather
   Fall faint upon your fiery sleep,
As on strange sands a strayed bird's feather
   The wind may choose to lose or keep.

But I, who leave my queen of panthers,
   As a tired honey-heavy bee
Gilt with sweet dust from gold-grained anthers
   Leaves the rose-chalice, what for me ?

From the ardours of the chaliced centre,
   From the amorous anthers' golden grime,
That scorch and smutch all wings that enter,
   I fly forth hot from honey-time.

But as to a bee's gilt thighs and winglets
   The flower-dust with the flower-smell clings ;
As a snake's mobile rampant ringlets
   Leave the sand marked with print of rings ;

So to my soul in surer fashion
   Your savage stamp and savour hangs ;
The print and perfume of old passion,
   The wild-beast mark of panther's fangs.

SESTINA

I SAW my soul at rest upon a day
  As a bird sleeping in the nest of night,
Among soft leaves that give the starlight way
  To touch its wings but not its eyes with light ;
So that it knew as one in visions may,
  And knew not as men waking, of delight.

This was the measure of my soul's delight ;
  It had no power of joy to fly by day,
Nor part in the large lordship of the light ;
  But in a secret moon-beholden way
Had all its will of dreams and pleasant night,
  And all the love and life that sleepers may.

But such life's triumph as men waking may
  It might not have to feed its faint delight
Between the stars by night and sun by day,
  Shut up with green leaves and a little light ;
Because its way was as a lost star's way,
  A world's not wholly known of day or night.

All loves and dreams and sounds and gleams of night
  Made it all music that such minstrels may,
And all they had they gave it of delight ;
  But in the full face of the fire of day
What place shall be for any starry light,
  What part of heaven in all the wide sun's way ?

Yet the soul woke not, sleeping by the way,
  Watched as a nursling of the large-eyed night,
And sought no strength nor knowledge of the day,
  Nor closer touch conclusive of delight,
Nor mightier joy nor truer than dreamers may,
  Nor more of song than they, nor more of light.

For who sleeps once and sees the secret light
  Whereby sleep shows the soul a fairer way
Between the rise and rest of day and night,
  Shall care no more to fare as all men may,
But be his place of pain or of delight,
  There shall he dwell, beholding night as day.

Song, have thy day and take thy fill of light
  Before the night be fallen across thy way;
Sing while he may, man hath no long delight.

THE YEAR OF THE ROSE

From the depths of the green garden-closes
Where the summer in darkness dozes
   Till autumn pluck from his hand
   An hour-glass that holds not a sand ;
From the maze that a flower-belt encloses
   To the stones and sea-grass on the strand
How red was the reign of the roses
   Over the rose-crowned land !

The year of the rose is brief ;
From the first blade blown to the sheaf,
   From the thin green leaf to the gold,
   It has time to be sweet and grow old,
To triumph and leave not a leaf
   For witness in winter's sight
   How lovers once in the light
Would mix their breath with its breath,
   And its spirit was quenched not of night,
As love is subdued not of death.

In the red-rose land not a mile
Of the meadows from stile to stile,
   Of the valleys from stream to stream,
   But the air was a long sweet dream
And the earth was a sweet wide smile

Red-mouthed of a goddess, returned
From the sea which had borne her and burned,
   That with one swift smile of her mouth
   Looked full on the north as it yearned,
And the north was more than the south.

For the north, when winter was long,
In his heart had made him a song,
   And clothed it with wings of desire,
   And shod it with shoon as of fire,
To carry the tale of his wrong
   To the south-west wind by the sea,
   That none might bear it but he
To the ear of the goddess unknown
   Who waits till her time shall be
To take the world for a throne.

In the earth beneath, and above
In the heaven where her name is love,
   She warms with light from her eyes
   The seasons of life as they rise,
And her eyes are as eyes of a dove,
   But the wings that lift her and bear
   As an eagle's, and all her hair
As fire by the wind's breath curled,
   And her passage is song through the air,
And her presence is spring through the world.

So turned she northward and came,
And the white-thorn land was aflame
   With the fires that were shed from her feet,
   That the north, by her love made sweet,
Should be called by a rose-red name ;

And a murmur was heard as of doves,
And a music beginning of loves
In the light that the roses made,
    Such light as the music loves,
The music of man with maid.

But the days drop one upon one,
And a chill soft wind is begun
    In the heart of the rose-red maze
    That weeps for the roseleaf days
And the reign of the rose undone
    That ruled so long in the light,
    And by spirit, and not by sight,
Through the darkness thrilled with its breath,
    Still ruled in the viewless night,
As love might rule over death.

The time of lovers is brief;
From the fair first joy to the grief
    That tells when love is grown old,
    From the warm wild kiss to the cold,
From the red to the white-rose leaf,
    They have but a season to seem
    As roseleaves lost on a stream
That part not and pass not apart
    As a spirit from dream to dream,
As a sorrow from heart to heart.

From the bloom and the gloom that encloses
The death-bed of Love where he dozes
    Till a relic be left not of sand
    To the hour-glass that breaks in his hand;
From the change in the grey garden-closes
    To the last stray grass of the strand,
A rain and ruin of roses
    Over the red-rose land

A WASTED VIGIL

I

COULDST thou not watch with me one hour? Behold,
Dawn skims the sea with flying feet of gold,
With sudden feet that graze the gradual sea;
    Couldst thou not watch with me?

II

What, not one hour? for star by star the night
Falls, and her thousands world by world take flight;
They die, and day survives, and what of thee?
    Couldst thou not watch with me?

III

Lo, far in heaven the web of night undone,
And on the sudden sea the gradual sun;
Wave to wave answers, tree responds to tree;
    Couldst thou not watch with me?

IV

Sunbeam by sunbeam creeps from line to line,
Foam by foam quickens on the brightening brine;
Sail by sail passes, flower by flower gets free;
    Couldst thou not watch with me?

V

Last year, a brief while since, an age ago,
A whole year past, with bud and bloom and snow,
O moon that wast in heaven, what friends were we !
    Couldst thou not watch with me ?

VI

Old moons, and last year's flowers, and last year's
        snows !
Who now saith to thee, moon ? or who saith, rose ?
O dust and ashes, once found fair to see !
    Couldst thou not watch with me ?

VII

O dust and ashes, once thought sweet to smell !
With me it is not, is it with thee well ?
O sea-drift blown from windward back to lee !
    Couldst thou not watch with me ?

VIII

The old year's dead hands are full of their dead flowers,
The old days are full of dead old loves of ours,
Born as a rose, and briefer born than she ;
    Couldst thou not watch with me ?

IX

Could two days live again of that dead year,
One would say, seeking us and passing here,
Where is she ? and one answering, *Where is he ?*
    Couldst thou not watch with me ?

X

Nay, those two lovers are not anywhere ;
If we were they, none knows us what we were,
Nor aught of all their barren grief and glee.
    Couldst thou not watch with me ?

XI

Half false, half fair, all feeble, be my verse
Upon thee not for blessing nor for curse ;
For some must stand, and some must fall or flee ;
    Couldst thou not watch with me ?

XII

As a new moon above spent stars thou wast ;
But stars endure after the moon is past.
Couldst thou not watch one hour, though I watch
    three ?
    Couldst thou not watch with me ?

XIII

What of the night ?   The night is full, the tide
Storms inland, the most ancient rocks divide ;
Yet some endure, and bow nor head nor knee ;
    Couldst thou not watch with me ?

XIV

Since thou art not as these are, go thy ways ;
Thou hast no part in all my nights and days.
Lie still, sleep on, be glad—as such things be ;
    Thou couldst not watch with me.

THE COMPLAINT OF LISA

(*Double Sestina*)

DECAMERON, X. 7

THERE is no woman living that draws breath
So sad as I, though all things sadden her.
There is not one upon life's weariest way
Who is weary as I am weary of all but death.
Toward whom I look as looks the sunflower
All day with all his whole soul toward the sun ;
While in the sun's sight I make moan all day,
And all night on my sleepless maiden bed
Weep and call out on death, O Love, and thee,
That thou or he would take me to the dead,
And know not what thing evil I have done
That life should lay such heavy hand on me.

Alas, Love, what is this thou wouldst with me ?
What honour shalt thou have to quench my breath,
Or what shall my heart broken profit thee ?
O Love, O great god Love, what have I done,
That thou shouldst hunger so after my death ?
My heart is harmless as my life's first day :
Seek out some false fair woman, and plague her
Till her tears even as my tears fill her bed :
I am the least flower in thy flowery way,

But till my time be come that I be dead
Let me live out my flower-time in the sun
Though my leaves shut before the sunflower.

O Love, Love, Love, the kingly sunflower!
Shall he the sun hath looked on look on me,
That live down here in shade, out of the sun,
Here living in the sorrow and shadow of death?
Shall he that feeds his heart full of the day
Care to give mine eyes light, or my lips breath?
Because she loves him shall my lord love her
Who is as a worm in my lord's kingly way?
I shall not see him or know him alive or dead;
But thou, I know thee, O Love, and pray to thee
That in brief while my brief life-days be done,
And the worm quickly make my marriage-bed.

For underground there is no sleepless bed:
But here since I beheld my sunflower
These eyes have slept not, seeing all night and day
His sunlike eyes, and face fronting the sun.
Wherefore if anywhere be any death,
I would fain find and fold him fast to me,
That I may sleep with the world's eldest dead,
With her that died seven centuries since, and her
That went last night down the night-wandering way.
For this is sleep indeed, when labour is done,
Without love, without dreams, and without breath,
And without thought, O name unnamed! of thee.

Ah, but, forgetting all things, shall I thee?
Wilt thou not be as now about my bed
There underground as here before the sun?
Shall not thy vision vex me alive and dead,

Thy moving vision without form or breath?
I read long since the bitter tale of her
Who read the tale of Launcelot on a day,
And died, and had no quiet after death,
But was moved ever along a weary way,
Lost with her love in the underworld; ah me,
O my king, O my lordly sunflower,
Would God to me too such a thing were done!

But if such sweet and bitter things be done,
Then, flying from life, I shall not fly from thee.
For in that living world without a sun
Thy vision will lay hold upon me dead,
And meet and mock me, and mar my peace in death.
Yet if being wroth God had such pity on her,
Who was a sinner and foolish in her day,
That even in hell they twain should breathe one
        breath,
Why should he not in some wise pity me?
So if I sleep not in my soft strait bed
I may look up and see my sunflower
As he the sun, in some divine strange way.

O poor my heart, well knowest thou in what way
This sore sweet evil unto us was done.
For on a holy and a heavy day
I was arisen out of my still small bed
To see the knights tilt, and one said to me
"The king," and seeing him, somewhat stopped my
        breath,
And if the girl spake more, I heard not her,
For only I saw what I shall see when dead,
A kingly flower of knights, a sunflower,

That shone against the sunlight like the sun,
And like a fire, O heart, consuming thee,
The fire of love that lights the pyre of death.

Howbeit I shall not die an evil death
Who have loved in such a sad and sinless way,
That this my love, lord, was no shame to thee.
So when mine eyes are shut against the sun,
O my soul's sun, O the world's sunflower,
Thou nor no man will quite despise me dead.
And dying I pray with all my low last breath
That thy whole life may be as was that day,
That feast-day that made trothplight death and me,
Giving the world light of thy great deeds done ;
And that fair face brightening thy bridal bed,
That God be good as God hath been to her.

That all things goodly and glad remain with her,
All things that make glad life and goodly death ;
That as a bee sucks from a sunflower
Honey, when summer draws delighted breath,
Her soul may drink of thy soul in like way,
And love make life a fruitful marriage-bed
Where day may bring forth fruits of joy to day
And night to night till days and nights be dead.
And as she gives light of her love to thee,
Give thou to her the old glory of days long done ;
And either give some heat of light to me,
To warm me where I sleep without the sun.

O sunflower made drunken with the sun,
O knight whose lady's heart draws thine to her,
Great king, glad lover, I have a word to thee.
There is a weed lives out of the sun's way,

Hid from the heat deep in the meadow's bed,
That swoons and whitens at the wind's least breath,
A flower star-shaped, that all a summer day
Will gaze her soul out on the sunflower
For very love till twilight finds her dead.
But the great sunflower heeds not her poor death,
Knows not when all her loving life is done ;
And so much knows my lord the king of me.

Aye, all day long he has no eye for me ;
With golden eye following the golden sun
From rose-coloured to purple-pillowed bed,
From birthplace to the flame-lit place of death,
From eastern end to western of his way.
So mine eye follows thee, my sunflower,
So the white star-flower turns and yearns to thee,
The sick weak weed, not well alive or dead,
Trod underfoot if any pass by her,
Pale, without colour of summer or summer breath
In the shrunk shuddering petals, that have done
No work but love, and die before the day.

But thou, to-day, to-morrow, and every day,
Be glad and great, O love whose love slays me.
Thy fervent flower made fruitful from the sun
Shall drop its golden seed in the world's way,
That all men thereof nourished shall praise thee
For grain and flower and fruit of works well done ;
Till thy shed seed, O shining sunflower,
Bring forth such growth of the world's garden-bed
As like the sun shall outlive age and death.
And yet I would thine heart had heed of her
Who loves thee alive ; but not till she be dead.
Come, Love, then, quickly, and take her utmost
        breath.

Song, speak for me who am dumb as are the dead ;
From my sad bed of tears I send forth thee,
To fly all day from sun's birth to sun's death
Down the sun's way after the flying sun,
For love of her that gave thee wings and breath,
Ere day be done, to seek the sunflower.

FOR THE FEAST OF GIORDANO BRUNO,

PHILOSOPHER AND MARTYR

I

Son of the lightning and the light that glows
    Beyond the lightning's or the morning's light,
    Soul splendid with all-righteous love of right,
In whose keen fire all hopes and fears and woes
Were clean consumed, and from their ashes rose
    Transfigured, and intolerable to sight
    Save of purged eyes whose lids had cast off night,
In love's and wisdom's likeness when they close,
Embracing, and between them truth stands fast,
    Embraced of either ; thou whose feet were set
    On English earth while this was England yet,
Our friend that art, our Sidney's friend that wast,
Heart hardier found and higher than all men's past,
    Shall we not praise thee though thine own forget ?

II

Lift up thy light on us and on thine own,
    O soul whose spirit on earth was as a rod
    To scourge off priests, a sword to pierce their
        God,
A staff for man's free thought to walk alone,

A lamp to lead him far from shrine and throne
    On ways untrodden where his fathers trod
    Ere earth's heart withered at a high priest's nod
And all men's mouths that made not prayer made
      moan.
From bonds and torments and the ravening flame
    Surely thy spirit of sense rose up to greet
    Lucretius, where such only spirits meet,
And walk with him apart till Shelley came
    To make the heaven of heavens more heavenly
      sweet
And mix with yours a third incorporate name.

AVE ATQUE VALE

IN MEMORY OF CHARLES BAUDELAIRE

Nous devrions pourtant lui porter quelques fleurs ;
Les morts, les pauvres morts, ont de grandes douleurs,
Et quand Octobre souffle, émondeur des vieux arbres,
Son vent mélancolique à l'entour de leurs marbres,
Certe, ils doivent trouver les vivants bien ingrats.

Les Fleurs du Mal.

I

SHALL I strew on thee rose or rue or laurel,
     Brother, on this that was the veil of thee ?
     Or quiet sea-flower moulded by the sea,
Or simplest growth of meadow-sweet or sorrel,
     Such as the summer-sleepy Dryads weave,
     Waked up by snow-soft sudden rains at eve ?
Or wilt thou rather, as on earth before,
     Half-faded fiery blossoms, pale with heat
     And full of bitter summer, but more sweet
To thee than gleanings of a northern shore
     Trod by no tropic feet ?

II

For always thee the fervid languid glories
     Allured of heavier suns in mightier skies ;
     Thine ears knew all the wandering watery sighs
Where the sea sobs round Lesbian promontories,

The barren kiss of piteous wave to wave
   That knows not where is that Leucadian grave
Which hides too deep the supreme head of song.
   Ah, salt and sterile as her kisses were,
   The wild sea winds her and the green gulfs bear
Hither and thither, and vex and work her wrong,
   Blind gods that cannot spare.

III

Thou sawest, in thine old singing season, brother,
   Secrets and sorrows unbeheld of us :
   Fierce loves, and lovely leaf-buds poisonous,
Bare to thy subtler eye, but for none other
   Blowing by night in some unbreathed-in clime ;
   The hidden harvest of luxurious time,
Sin without shape, and pleasure without speech ;
   And where strange dreams in a tumultuous sleep
   Make the shut eyes of stricken spirits weep ;
And with each face thou sawest the shadow on each,
   Seeing as men sow men reap.

IV

O sleepless heart and sombre soul unsleeping,
   That were athirst for sleep and no more life
   And no more love, for peace and no more strife !
Now the dim gods of death have in their keeping
   Spirit and body and all the springs of song,
   Is it well now where love can do no wrong,
Where stingless pleasure has no foam or fang
   Behind the unopening closure of her lips ?
   Is it not well where soul from body slips
And flesh from bone divides without a pang
   As dew from flower-bell drips ?

E 2

V

It is enough ; the end and the beginning
  Are one thing to thee, who art past the end.
  O hand unclasped of unbeholden friend,
For thee no fruits to pluck, no palms for winning,
  No triumph and no labour and no lust,
  Only dead yew-leaves and a little dust.
O quiet eyes wherein the light saith nought,
  Whereto the day is dumb, nor any night
  With obscure finger silences your sight,
Nor in your speech the sudden soul speaks thought,
  Sleep, and have sleep for light.

VI

Now all strange hours and all strange loves are over,
  Dreams and desires and sombre songs and sweet,
  Hast thou found place at the great knees and
   feet
Of some pale Titan-woman like a lover,
  Such as thy vision here solicited,
  Under the shadow of her fair vast head,
The deep division of prodigious breasts,
  The solemn slope of mighty limbs asleep,
  The weight of awful tresses that still keep
The savour and shade of old-world pine-forests
  Where the wet hill-winds weep ?

VII

Hast thou found any likeness for thy vision ?
  O gardener of strange flowers, what bud, what
   bloom,
  Hast thou found sown, what gathered in the
   gloom ?
What of despair, of rapture, of derision,

What of life is there, what of ill or good?
Are the fruits grey like dust or bright like blood?
Does the dim ground grow any seed of ours,
The faint fields quicken any terrene root,
In low lands where the sun and moon are mute
And all the stars keep silence? Are there flowers
At all, or any fruit?

VIII

Alas, but though my flying song flies after,
O sweet strange elder singer, thy more fleet
Singing, and footprints of thy fleeter feet,
Some dim derision of mysterious laughter
From the blind tongueless warders of the dead,
Some gainless glimpse of Proserpine's veiled
head,
Some little sound of unregarded tears
Wept by effaced unprofitable eyes,
And from pale mouths some cadence of dead
sighs—
These only, these the hearkening spirit hears,
Sees only such things rise.

IX

Thou art far too far for wings of words to follow,
Far too far off for thought or any prayer.
What ails us with thee, who art wind and air?
What ails us gazing where all seen is hollow?
Yet with some fancy, yet with some desire,
Dreams pursue death as winds a flying fire,
Our dreams pursue our dead and do not find.

Still, and more swift than they, the thin flame
    flies,
    The low light fails us in elusive skies,
Still the foiled earnest ear is deaf, and blind
    Are still the eluded eyes.

X

Not thee, O never thee, in all time's changes,
    Not thee, but this the sound of thy sad soul,
    The shadow of thy swift spirit, this shut scroll
I lay my hand on, and not death estranges
    My spirit from communion of thy song—
    These memories and these melodies that throng
Veiled porches of a Muse funereal—
    These I salute, these touch, these clasp and fold
    As though a hand were in my hand to hold,
Or through mine ears a mourning musical
    Of many mourners rolled.

XI

I among these, I also, in such station
    As when the pyre was charred, and piled the
      sods,
    And offering to the dead made, and their gods,
The old mourners had, standing to make libation,
    I stand, and to the gods and to the dead
    Do reverence without prayer or praise, and shed
Offering to these unknown, the gods of gloom,
    And what of honey and spice my seedlands bear,
    And what I may of fruits in this chilled air,
And lay, Orestes-like, across the tomb
    A curl of severed hair.

XII

But by no hand nor any treason stricken,
    Not like the low-lying head of Him, the King,
    The flame that made of Troy a ruinous thing,
Thou liest, and on this dust no tears could quicken
    There fall no tears like theirs that all men hear
    Fall tear by sweet imperishable tear
Down the opening leaves of holy poets' pages.
    Thee not Orestes, not Electra mourns ;
    But bending us-ward with memorial urns
The most high Muses that fulfil all ages
    Weep, and our God's heart yearns.

XIII

For, sparing of his sacred strength, not often
    Among us darkling here the lord of light
    Makes manifest his music and his might
In hearts that open and in lips that soften
    With the soft flame and heat of songs that shine.
    Thy lips indeed he touched with bitter wine,
And nourished them indeed with bitter bread ;
    Yet surely from his hand thy soul's food came,
    The fire that scarred thy spirit at his flame
Was lighted, and thine hungering heart he fed
    Who feeds our hearts with fame.

XIV

Therefore he too now at thy soul's sunsetting,
    God of all suns and songs, he too bends down
    To mix his laurel with thy cypress crown,
And save thy dust from blame and from forgetting.

Therefore he too, seeing all thou wert and art,
    Compassionate, with sad and sacred heart,
Mourns thee of many his children the last dead,
        And hallows with strange tears and alien sighs
        Thine unmelodious mouth and sunless eyes,
And over thine irrevocable head
        Sheds light from the under skies.

XV

And one weeps with him in the ways Lethean,
        And stains with tears her changing bosom chill:
        That obscure Venus of the hollow hill,
That thing transformed which was the Cytherean,
        With lips that lost their Grecian laugh divine
        Long since, and face no more called Erycine;
A ghost, a bitter and luxurious god.
        Thee also with fair flesh and singing spell
        Did she, a sad and second prey, compel
Into the footless places once more trod,
        And shadows hot from hell.

XVI

And now no sacred staff shall break in blossom,
        No choral salutation lure to light
        A spirit sick with perfume and sweet night
And love's tired eyes and hands and barren bosom.
        There is no help for these things; none to mend
        And none to mar; not all our songs, O friend,
Will make death clear or make life durable.
        Howbeit with rose and ivy and wild vine
        And with wild notes about this dust of thine
At least I fill the place where white dreams dwell
        And wreathe an unseen shrine.

XVII

Sleep ; and if life was bitter to thee, pardon,
 If sweet, give thanks ; thou hast no more to
  live ;
 And to give thanks is good, and to forgive.
Out of the mystic and the mournful garden
 Where all day through thine hands in barren
  braid
 Wove the sick flowers of secrecy and shade,
Green buds of sorrow and sin, and remnants grey,
 Sweet-smelling, pale with poison, sanguine-
  hearted,
 Passions that sprang from sleep and thoughts
  that started,
Shall death not bring us all as thee one day
 Among the days departed ?

XVIII

For thee, O now a silent soul, my brother,
 Take at my hands this garland, and farewell.
 Thin is the leaf, and chill the wintry smell,
And chill the solemn earth, a fatal mother,
 With sadder than the Niobean womb,
 And in the hollow of her breasts a tomb.
Content thee, howsoe'er, whose days are done ;
 There lies not any troublous thing before,
 Nor sight nor sound to war against thee more,
For whom all winds are quiet as the sun,
 All waters as the shore.

MEMORIAL VERSES

ON THE DEATH OF THÉOPHILE GAUTIER

DEATH, what hast thou to do with me? So saith
Love, with eyes set against the face of Death;
    What have I done, O thou strong Death, to thee,
That mine own lips should wither from thy breath?

Though thou be blind as fire or as the sea,
Why should thy waves and storms make war on me?
    Is it for hate thou hast to find me fair,
Or for desire to kiss, if it might be,

My very mouth of song, and kill me there?
So with keen rains vexing his crownless hair,
    · With bright feet bruised from no delightful way,
Through darkness and the disenchanted air,

Lost Love went weeping half a winter's day.
And the armèd wind that smote him seemed to say,
    How shall the dew live when the dawn is fled,
Or wherefore should the Mayflower outlast May?

Then Death took Love by the right hand and said,
Smiling: Come now and look upon thy dead.
    But Love cast down the glories of his eyes,
And bowed down like a flower his flowerless head.

And Death spake, saying : What ails thee in such
 wise,
Being god, to shut thy sight up from the skies ?
 If thou canst see not, hast thou ears to hear ?
Or is thy soul too as a leaf that dies ?

Even as he spake with fleshless lips of fear,
But soft as sleep sings in a tired man's ear,
 Behold, the winter was not, and its might
Fell, and fruits broke forth of the barren year.

And upon earth was largess of great light,
And moving music winged for worldwide flight,
 And shapes and sounds of gods beheld and heard,
And day's foot set upon the neck of night.

And with such song the hollow ways were stirred
As of a god's heart hidden in a bird,
 Or as the whole soul of the sun in spring
Should find full utterance in one flower-soft word,

And all the season should break forth and sing
From one flower's lips, in one rose triumphing ;
 Such breath and light of song as of a flame
Made ears and spirits of them that heard it ring.

And Love beholding knew not for the same
The shape that led him, nor in face nor name,
 For he was bright and great of thews and fair,
And in Love's eyes he was not Death, but Fame.

Not that grey ghost whose life is empty and bare
And his limbs moulded out of mortal air,
 A cloud of change that shifts into a shower
And dies and leaves no light for time to wear :

But a god clothed with his own joy and power,
A god re-risen out of his mortal hour
   Immortal, king and lord of time and space,
With eyes that look on them as from a tower.

And where he stood the pale sepulchral place
Bloomed, as new life might in a bloodless face,
   And where men sorrowing came to seek a tomb
With funeral flowers and tears for grief and grace,

They saw with light as of a world in bloom
The portal of the House of Fame illume
   The ways of life wherein we toiling tread,
And watched the darkness as a brand consume.

And through the gates where rule the deathless dead
The sound of a new singer's soul was shed
   That sang among his kinsfolk, and a beam
Shot from the star on a new ruler's head.

A new star lighting the Lethean stream,
A new song mixed into the song supreme
   Made of all souls of singers and their might,
That makes of life and time and death a dream.

Thy star, thy song, O soul that in our sight
Wast as a sun that made for man's delight
   Flowers and all fruits in season, being so near
The sun-god's face, our god that gives us light.

To him of all gods that we love or fear
Thou amongst all men by thy name wast dear,
   Dear to the god that gives us spirit of song
To bind and burn all hearts of men that hear.

The god that makes men's words too sweet and strong
For life or time or death to do them wrong,
   Who sealed with his thy spirit for a sign
And filled it with his breath thy whole life long.

Who made thy moist lips fiery with new wine
Pressed from the grapes of song, the sovereign vine,
   And with all love of all things loveliest
Gave thy soul power to make them more divine.

That thou might'st breathe upon the breathless rest
Of marble, till the brows and lips and breast
   Felt fall from off them as a cancelled curse
That speechless sleep wherewith they lived opprest.

Who gave thee strength and heat of spirit to pierce
All clouds of form and colour that disperse,
   And leave the spirit of beauty to remould
In types of clean chryselephantine verse.

Who gave thee words more golden than fine gold
To carve in shapes more glorious than of old,
   And build thy songs up in the sight of time
As statues set in godhead manifold:

In sight and scorn of temporal change and clime
That meet the sun re-risen with refluent rhyme
   —As god to god might answer face to face—
From lips whereon the morning strikes sublime.

Dear to the god, our god who gave thee place
Among the chosen of days, the royal race,
   The lords of light, whose eyes of old and ears
Saw even on earth and heard him for a space.

There are the souls of those once mortal years
That wrought with fire of joy and light of tears
    In words divine as deeds that grew thereof
Such music as he swoons with love who hears.

There are the lives that lighten from above
Our under lives, the spheral souls that move
    Through the ancient heaven of song-illumined air
Whence we that hear them singing die with love.

There all the crowned Hellenic heads, and there
The old gods who made men godlike as they were,
    The lyric lips wherefrom all songs take fire,
Live eyes, and light of Apollonian hair.

There, round the sovereign passion of that lyre
Which the stars hear and tremble with desire,
    The ninefold light Pierian is made one
That here we see divided, and aspire,

Seeing, after this or that crown to be won ;
But where they hear the singing of the sun,
    All form, all sound, all colour, and all thought
Are as one body and soul in unison.

There the song sung shines as a picture wrought,
The painted mouths sing that on earth say nought,
    The carven limbs have sense of blood and growth
And large-eyed life that seeks nor lacks not aught.

There all the music of thy living mouth
Lives, and all loves wrought of thine hand in youth
    And bound about the breasts and brows with gold
And coloured pale or dusk from north or south.

Fair living things made to thy will of old,
Born of thy lips, no births of mortal mould,
   That in the world of song about thee wait
Where thought and truth are one and manifold.

Within the graven lintels of the gate
That here divides our vision and our fate,
   The dreams we walk in and the truths of sleep,
All sense and spirit have life inseparate.

There what one thinks, is his to grasp and keep ;
There are no dreams, but very joys to reap,
   No foiled desires that die before delight,
No fears to see across our joys and weep.

There hast thou all thy will of thought and sight,
All hope for harvest, and all heaven for flight ;
   The sunrise of whose golden-mouthed glad head
To paler songless ghosts was heat and light.

Here where the sunset of our year is red
Men think of thee as of the summer dead,
   Gone forth before the snows, before thy day,
With unshod feet, with brows unchapleted.

Couldst thou not wait till age had wound, they say,
Round those wreathed brows his soft white blossoms ?
    Nay,
   Why shouldst thou vex thy soul with this harsh air,
Thy bright-winged soul, once free to take its way ?

Nor for men's reverence hadst thou need to wear
The holy flower of grey time-hallowed hair ;
   Nor were it fit that aught of thee grew old,
Fair lover all thy days of all things fair.

And hear we not thy words of molten gold
Singing? or is their light and heat acold
   Whereat men warmed their spirits?   Nay, for all
These yet are with us, ours to hear and hold.

The lovely laughter, the clear tears, the call
Of love to love on ways where shadows fall,
   Through doors of dim division and disguise,
And music made of doubts unmusical;

The love that caught strange light from death's own
        eyes,[1]
And filled death's lips with fiery words and sighs,
   And half asleep let feed from veins of his
Her close red warm snake's mouth, Egyptian-wise:

And that great night of love more strange than this,[2]
When she that made the whole world's bale and bliss
   Made king of all the world's desire a slave,
And killed him in mid kingdom with a kiss;

Veiled loves that shifted shapes and shafts, and gave,[3]
Laughing, strange gifts to hands that durst not crave,
   Flowers double-blossomed, fruits of scent and hue
Sweet as the bride-bed, stranger than the grave;

All joys and wonders of old lives and new
That ever in love's shine or shadow grew,
   And all the grief whereof he dreams and grieves,
And all sweet roots fed on his light and dew;

[1] *La Morte Amoureuse.*
[2] *Une Nuit de Cléopâtre.*   [3] *Mademoiselle de Maupin.*

All these through thee our spirit of sense perceives,
As threads in the unseen woof thy music weaves,
  Birds caught and snared that fill our ears with thee,
Bay-blossoms in thy wreath of brow-bound leaves.

Mixed with the masque of death's old comedy
Though thou too pass, have here our flowers, that we
  For all the flowers thou gav'st upon thee shed,
And pass not crownless to Persephone.

Blue lotus-blooms and white and rosy-red
We wind with poppies for thy silent head,
  And on this margin of the sundering sea
Leave thy sweet light to rise upon the dead.

SONNET

(WITH A COPY OF *Mademoiselle de Maupin*)

THIS is the golden book of spirit and sense,
  The holy writ of beauty ; he that wrought
  Made it with dreams and faultless words and
   thought
That seeks and finds and loses in the dense
Dim air of life that beauty's excellence
  Wherewith love makes one hour of life distraught
  And all hours after follow and find not aught.
Here is that height of all love's eminence
Where man may breathe but for a breathing-space
  And feel his soul burn as an altar-fire
  To the unknown God of unachieved desire,
And from the middle mystery of the place
  Watch lights that break, hear sounds as of a
   quire,
But see not twice unveiled the veiled God's face.

AGE AND SONG

(TO BARRY CORNWALL)

I

In vain men tell us time can alter
Old loves or make old memories falter,
  That with the old year the old year's life closes.
The old dew still falls on the old sweet flowers,
The old sun revives the new-fledged hours,
  The old summer rears the new-born roses.

II

Much more a Muse that bears upon her
Raiment and wreath and flower of honour,
  Gathered long since and long since woven,
Fades not or falls as fall the vernal
Blossoms that bear no fruit eternal,
  By summer or winter charred or cloven.

III

No time casts down, no time upraises,
Such loves, such memories, and such praises,
  As need no grace of sun or shower,
No saving screen from frost or thunder
To tend and house around and under
  The imperishable and fearless flower.

F 2

IV

Old thanks, old thoughts, old aspirations,
Outlive men's lives and lives of nations,
   Dead, but for one thing which survives—
The inalienable and unpriced treasure,
The old joy of power, the old pride of pleasure,
   That lives in light above men's lives.

IN MEMORY OF BARRY CORNWALL

(OCTOBER 4, 1874)

I

IN the garden of death, where the singers whose
    names are deathless
  One with another make music unheard of men,
Where the dead sweet roses fade not of lips long
    breathless,
    And the fair eyes shine that shall weep not or
    change again,
Who comes now crowned with the blossom of snow-
    white years?
What music is this that the world of the dead men
    hears?

II

Beloved of men, whose words on our lips were
    honey,
  Whose name in our ears and our fathers' ears was
    sweet,
Like summer gone forth of the land his songs made
    sunny,
  To the beautiful veiled bright world where the glad
    ghosts meet,
Child, father, bridegroom and bride, and anguish
    and rest,
No soul shall pass of a singer than this more blest.

III

Blest for the years' sweet sake that were filled and
 brightened,
  As a forest with birds, with the fruit and the flower
  of his song ;
For the souls' sake blest that heard, and their cares
 were lightened,
  For the hearts' sake blest that have fostered his
  name so long ;
By the living and dead lips blest that have loved his
 name,
And clothed with their praise and crowned with their
 love for fame.

IV

Ah, fair and fragrant his fame as flowers that close
 not,
  That shrink not by day for heat or for cold by
  night,
As a thought in the heart shall increase when the
 heart's self knows not,
  Shall endure in our ears as a sound, in our eyes as
  a light ;
Shall wax with the years that wane and the seasons'
 chime,
As a white rose thornless that grows in the garden
 of time.

V

The same year calls, and one goes hence with
 another,
  And men sit sad that were glad for their sweet
  songs' sake ;

The same year beckons, and elder with younger
  brother
  Takes mutely the cup from his hand that we all
    shall take.[1]
They pass ere the leaves be past or the snows be
  come ;
And the birds are loud, but the lips that outsang them
  dumb.

VI

Time takes them home that we loved, fair names and
  famous,
  To the soft long sleep, to the broad sweet bosom
    of death ;
But the flower of their souls he shall take not away
  to shame us,
  Nor the lips lack song for ever that now lack
    breath.
For with us shall the music and perfume that die not
  dwell,
Though the dead to our dead bid welcome, and we
  farewell.

[1] Sydney Dobell died August 22, 1874.

EPICEDE

(James Lorimer Graham died at Florence, April 30, 1876)

LIFE may give for love to death
   Little ; what are life's gifts worth
   To the dead wrapt round with earth?
Yet from lips of living breath
   Sighs or words we are fain to give,
   All that yet, while yet we live,
Life may give for love to death.

Dead so long before his day,
   Passed out of the Italian sun
   To the dark where all is done,
Fallen upon the verge of May ;
   Here at life's and April's end
   How should song salute my friend
Dead so long before his day ?

Not a kindlier life or sweeter
   Time, that lights and quenches men,
   Now may quench or light again,
Mingling with the mystic metre
   Woven of all men's lives with his
   Not a clearer note than this,
Not a kindlier life or sweeter.

In this heavenliest part of earth
  He that living loved the light,
  Light and song, may rest aright,
One in death, if strange in birth,
  With the deathless dead that make
  Life the lovelier for their sake
In this heavenliest part of earth.

Light, and song, and sleep at last—
  Struggling hands and suppliant knees
  Get no goodlier gift than these.
Song that holds remembrance fast,
  Light that lightens death, attend
  Round their graves who have to friend
Light, and song, and sleep at last.

TO VICTOR HUGO

He had no children, who for love of men,
 Being God, endured of Gods such things as thou,
 Father ; nor on his thunder-beaten brow
Fell such a woe as bows thine head again,
Twice bowed before, though godlike, in man's ken,
 And seen too high for any stroke to bow
 Save this of some strange God's that bends it now
The third time with such weight as bruised it then.
Fain would grief speak, fain utter for love's sake
Some word ; but comfort who might bid thee take ?
 What God in your own tongue shall talk with thee,
Showing how all souls that look upon the sun
Shall be for thee one spirit and thy son,
 And thy soul's child the soul of man to be ?

 January 3, 1876.

INFERIAE

SPRING, and the light and sound of things on earth
Requickening, all within our green sea's girth ;
A time of passage or a time of birth
   Fourscore years since as this year, first and last.

The sun is all about the world we see,
The breath and strength of very spring ; and we
Live, love, and feed on our own hearts ; but he
   Whose heart fed mine has passed into the past.

Past, all things born with sense and blood and breath ;
The flesh hears nought that now the spirit saith.
If death be like as birth and birth as death,
   The first was fair—more fair should be the last.

Fourscore years since, and come but one month more
The count were perfect of his mortal score
Whose sail went seaward yesterday from shore
   To cross the last of many an unsailed sea.

Light, love and labour up to life's last height,
These three were stars unsetting in his sight ;
Even as the sun is life and heat and light
   And sets not nor is dark when dark are we.

The life, the spirit, and the work were one
That here—ah, who shall say, that here are done?
Not I, that know not; father, not thy son,
   For all the darkness of the night and sea.

March 5, 1877

A BIRTH-SONG

(For Olivia Frances Madox Rossetti, born September 20, 1875)

OUT of the dark sweet sleep
Where no dreams laugh or weep
  Borne through bright gates of birth
Into the dim sweet light
Where day still dreams of night
  While heaven takes form on earth,
White rose of spirit and flesh, red lily of love,
  What note of song have we
  Fit for the birds and thee,
Fair nestling couched beneath the mother-dove?

Nay, in some more divine
Small speechless song of thine
  Some news too good for words,
Heart-hushed and smiling, we
Might hope to have of thee,
  The youngest of God's birds,
If thy sweet sense might mix itself with ours,
  If ours might understand
  The language of thy land,
Ere thine become the tongue of mortal hours:

Ere thy lips learn too soon
Their soft first human tune,
   Sweet, but less sweet than now,
And thy raised eyes to read
Glad and good things indeed,
   But none so sweet as thou :
Ere thought lift up their flower-soft lids to see
   What life and love on earth
   Bring thee for gifts at birth,
But none so good as thine who hast given us thee :

   Now, ere thy sense forget
   The heaven that fills it yet,
      Now, sleeping or awake,
   If thou couldst tell, or we
   Ask and be heard of thee,
      For love's undying sake,
From thy dumb lips divine and bright mute speech
   Such news might touch our ear
   That then would burn to hear
Too high a message now for man's to reach.

   Ere the gold hair of corn
   Had withered wast thou born,
      To make the good time glad ;
   The time that but last year
   Fell colder than a tear
      On hearts and hopes turned sad,
High hopes and hearts requickening in thy dawn,
   Even theirs whose life-springs, child,
   Filled thine with life and smiled,
But then wept blood for half their own withdrawn.[1]

---

[1] Oliver Madox Brown died November 5, 1874, in his twentieth year.

If death and birth be one,
And set with rise of sun,
  And truth with dreams divine,
Some word might come with thee
From over the still sea
  Deep hid in shade or shine,
Crossed by the crossing sails of death and birth,
  Word of some sweet new thing
  Fit for such lips to bring,
Some word of love, some afterthought of earth.

If love be strong as death,
By what so natural breath
  As thine could this be said?
By what so lovely way
Could love send word to say
  He lives and is not dead?
Such word alone were fit for only thee,
  If his and thine have met
  Where spirits rise and set,
His whom we see not, thine whom scarce we see:

His there new-born, as thou
New-born among us now;
  His, here so fruitful-souled,
Now veiled and silent here,
Now dumb as thou last year,
  A ghost of one year old:
If lights that change their sphere in changing meet,
  Some ray might his not give
  To thine who wast to live,
And make thy present with his past life sweet?

Let dreams that laugh or weep,
All glad and sad dreams, sleep;

Truth more than dreams is dear.
Let thoughts that change and fly,
Sweet thoughts and swift, go by ;
More than all thought is here.
More than all hope can forge or memory feign
The life that in our eyes,
Made out of love's life, lies,
And flower-like fed with love for sun and rain.

Twice royal in its root
The sweet small olive-shoot
Here set in sacred earth ;
Twice dowered with glorious grace
From either heaven-born race
First blended in its birth ;
Fair God or Genius of so fair an hour,
For love of either name
Twice crowned, with love and fame,
Guard and be gracious to the fair-named flower.

October 19, 1875.

EX-VOTO

WHEN their last hour shall rise
Pale on these mortal eyes,
Herself like one that dies,
    And kiss me dying
The cold last kiss, and fold
Close round my limbs her cold
Soft shade as raiment rolled
    And leave them lying,

If aught my soul would say
Might move to hear me pray
The birth-god of my day
    That he might hearken,
This grace my heart should crave,
To find no landward grave
That worldly springs make brave,
    World's winters darken,

Nor grow through gradual hours
The cold blind seed of flowers
Made by new beams and showers
    From limbs that moulder,
Nor take my part with earth,
But find for death's new birth
A bed of larger girth,
    More chaste and colder.

Not earth's for spring and fall,
Not earth's at heart, not all
Earth's making, though men call
   Earth only mother,
Not hers at heart she bare
Me, but thy child, O fair
Sea, and thy brother's care,
   The wind thy brother.

Yours was I born, and ye,
The sea-wind and the sea,
Made all my soul in me
   A song for ever,
A harp to string and smite
For love's sake of the bright
Wind and the sea's delight,
   To fail them never :

Not while on this side death
I hear what either saith
And drink of either's breath
   With heart's thanksgiving
That in my veins like wine
Some sharp salt blood of thine,
Some springtide pulse of brine,
   Yet leaps up living.

When thy salt lips wellnigh
Sucked in my mouth's last sigh,
Grudged I so much to die
   This death as others ?
Was it no ease to think
The chalice from whose brink
Fate gave me death to drink
   Was thine—my mother's ?

Thee too, the all-fostering earth,
Fair as thy fairest birth,
More than thy worthiest worth,
    We call, we know thee,
More sweet and just and dread
Than live men highest of head
Or even thy holiest dead
    Laid low below thee.

The sunbeam on the sheaf,
The dewfall on the leaf,
All joy, all grace, all grief,
    Are thine for giving;
Of thee our loves are born,
Our lives and loves, that mourn
And triumph; tares with corn,
    Dead seed with living:

All good and ill things done
In eyeshot of the sun
At last in thee made one
    Rest well contented;
All words of all man's breath
And works he doth or saith,
All wholly done to death,
    None long lamented.

A slave to sons of thee,
Thou, seeming, yet art free:
But who shall make the sea
    Serve even in seeming?
What plough shall bid it bear
Seed to the sun and the air,
Fruit for thy strong sons' fare,
    Fresh wine's foam streaming?

What oldworld son of thine,
Made drunk with death as wine,
Hath drunk the bright sea's brine
   With lips of laughter ?
Thy blood they drink ; but he
Who hath drunken of the sea
Once deeplier than of thee
   Shall drink not after.

Of thee thy sons of men
Drink deep, and thirst again ;
For wine in feasts, and then
   In fields for slaughter ;
But thirst shall touch not him
Who hath felt with sense grown dim
Rise, covering lip and limb,
   The wan sea's water.

All fire of thirst that aches
The salt sea cools and slakes
More than all springs or lakes,
   Freshets or shallows ;
Wells where no beam can burn
Through frondage of the fern
That hides from hart and hern
   The haunt it hallows.

Peace with all graves on earth
For death or sleep or birth
Be alway, one in worth
   One with another ;
But when my time shall be,
O mother, O my sea,
Alive or dead, take me,
   Me too, my mother.

A BALLAD OF DREAMLAND

I HID my heart in a nest of roses,
　Out of the sun's way, hidden apart ;
In a softer bed than the soft white snow's is,
　Under the roses I hid my heart.
　Why would it sleep not ? why should it start,
When never a leaf of the rose-tree stirred ?
　What made sleep flutter his wings and part ?
Only the song of a secret bird.

Lie still, I said, for the wind's wing closes,
　And mild leaves muffle the keen sun's dart ;
Lie still, for the wind on the warm sea dozes,
　And the wind is unquieter yet than thou art.
　Does a thought in thee still as a thorn's wound
　　smart ?
Does the fang still fret thee of hope deferred ?
　What bids the lids of thy sleep dispart ?
Only the song of a secret bird.

The green land's name that a charm encloses,
　It never was writ in the traveller's chart,
And sweet on its trees as the fruit that grows is,
　It never was sold in the merchant's mart.
　The swallows of dreams through its dim fields
　　dart,

And sleep's are the tunes in its tree-tops heard ;
    No hound's note wakens the wildwood hart,
Only the song of a secret bird.

ENVOI

In the world of dreams I have chosen my part,
    To sleep for a season and hear no word
Of true love's truth or of light love's art,
    Only the song of a secret bird.

CYRIL TOURNEUR

A SEA that heaves with horror of the night,
 As maddened by the moon that hangs aghast
 With strain and torment of the ravening blast,
Haggard as hell, a bleak blind bloody light ;
No shore but one red reef of rock in sight,
 Whereon the waifs of many a wreck were cast
 And shattered in the fierce nights overpast
Wherein more souls toward hell than heaven took
 flight ;
And 'twixt the shark-toothed rocks and swallowing
 shoals
A cry as out of hell from all these souls
 Sent through the sheer gorge of the slaughtering
  sea,
Whose thousand throats, full-fed with life by death,
Fill the black air with foam and furious breath ;
 And over all these one star—Chastity.

A BALLAD OF FRANÇOIS VILLON

PRINCE OF ALL BALLAD-MAKERS

BIRD of the bitter bright grey golden morn
   Scarce risen upon the dusk of dolorous years,
First of us all and sweetest singer born
    Whose far shrill note the world of new men hears
    Cleave the cold shuddering shade as twilight
      clears ;
When song new-born put off the old world's attire
And felt its tune on her changed lips expire,
   Writ foremost on the roll of them that came
Fresh girt for service of the latter lyre,
    Villon, our sad bad glad mad brother's name !

Alas the joy, the sorrow, and the scorn,
   That clothed thy life with hopes and sins and fears,
And gave thee stones for bread and tares for corn
    And plume-plucked gaol-birds for thy starveling
      peers
    Till death clipt close their flight with shameful
      shears ;
Till shifts came short and loves were hard to hire,
When lilt of song nor twitch of twangling wire
   Could buy thee bread or kisses ; when light fame
Spurned like a ball and haled through brake and
    briar,
    Villon, our sad bad glad mad brother's name !

Poor splendid wings so frayed and soiled and torn !
  Poor kind wild eyes so dashed with light quick
      tears !
Poor perfect voice, most blithe when most forlorn,
  That rings athwart the sea whence no man steers
  Like joy-bells crossed with death-bells in our ears !
What far delight has cooled the fierce desire
That like some ravenous bird was strong to tire
  On that frail flesh and soul consumed with flame,
But left more sweet than roses to respire,
  Villon, our sad bad glad mad brother's name ?

ENVOI

Prince of sweet songs made out of tears and fire,
A harlot was thy nurse, a God thy sire ;
  Shame soiled thy song, and song assoiled thy
      shame.
But from thy feet now death has washed the mire,
Love reads out first at head of all our quire,
  Villon, our sad bad glad mad brother's name.

PASTICHE

Now the days are all gone over
Of our singing, love by lover,
Days of summer-coloured seas
Blown adrift through beam and breeze.

Now the nights are all past over
Of our dreaming, dreams that hover
In a mist of fair false things,
Nights afloat on wide wan wings.

Now the loves with faith for mother,
Now the fears with hope for brother,
Scarce are with us as strange words,
Notes from songs of last year's birds.

Now all good that comes or goes is
As the smell of last year's roses,
As the radiance in our eyes
Shot from summer's ere he dies.

Now the morning faintlier risen
Seems no God come forth of prison,
But a bird of plume-plucked wing,
Pale with thoughts of evening.

Now hath hope, outraced in running,
Given the torch up of his cunning
And the palm he thought to wear
Even to his own strong child—despair.

BEFORE SUNSET

In the lower lands of day
  On the hither side of night,
There is nothing that will stay,
  There are all things soft to sight ;
  Lighted shade and shadowy light
In the wayside and the way,
  Hours the sun has spared to smite,
Flowers the rain has left to play.

Shall these hours run down and say
  No good thing of thee and me ?
Time that made us and will slay
  Laughs at love in me and thee ;
  But if here the flowers may see
One whole hour of amorous breath,
  Time shall die, and love shall be
Lord as time was over death.

SONG

Love laid his sleepless head
On a thorny rosy bed ;
And his eyes with tears were red,
And pale his lips as the dead.

And fear and sorrow and scorn
Kept watch by his head forlorn,
Till the night was overworn
And the world was merry with morn.

And Joy came up with the day
And kissed Love's lips as he lay,
And the watchers ghostly and grey
Sped from his pillow away.

And his eyes as the dawn grew bright,
And his lips waxed ruddy as light :
Sorrow may reign for a night,
But day shall bring back delight.

A VISION OF SPRING IN WINTER

I

O TENDER time that love thinks long to see,
    Sweet foot of spring that with her footfall sows
    Late snowlike flowery leavings of the snows,
Be not too long irresolute to be ;
O mother-month, where have they hidden thee ?
    Out of the pale time of the flowerless rose
I reach my heart out toward the springtime lands,
    I stretch my spirit forth to the fair hours,
        The purplest of the prime ;
I lean my soul down over them, with hands
    Made wide to take the ghostly growths of flowers ;
        I send my love back to the lovely time.

II

Where has the greenwood hid thy gracious head ?
    Veiled with what visions while the grey world
        grieves,
    Or muffled with what shadows of green leaves,
What warm intangible green shadows spread
To sweeten the sweet twilight for thy bed ?
    What sleep enchants thee ? what delight deceives ?

Where the deep dreamlike dew before the dawn
  Feels not the fingers of the sunlight yet
    Its silver web unweave,
Thy footless ghost on some unfooted lawn
  Whose air the unrisen sunbeams fear to fret
    Lives a ghost's life of daylong dawn and eve.

III

Sunrise it sees not, neither set of star,
  Large nightfall, nor imperial plenilune,
    Nor strong sweet shape of the full-breasted noon ;
But where the silver-sandalled shadows are,
Too soft for arrows of the sun to mar,
  Moves with the mild gait of an ungrown moon :
Hard overhead the half-lit crescent swims,
  The tender-coloured night draws hardly breath,
    The light is listening ;
They watch the dawn of slender-shapen limbs,
  Virginal, born again of doubtful death,
    Chill foster-father of the weanling spring.

IV

As sweet desire of day before the day,
  As dreams of love before the true love born,
    From the outer edge of winter overworn
The ghost arisen of May before the May
Takes through dim air her unawakened way,
  The gracious ghost of morning risen ere morn.
With little unblown breasts and child-eyed looks
  Following, the very maid, the girl-child spring,
    Lifts windward her bright brows,
Dips her light feet in warm and moving brooks,
  And kindles with her own mouth's colouring
    The fearful firstlings of the plumeless boughs.

V

I seek thee sleeping, and awhile I see,
   Fair face that art not, how thy maiden breath
   Shall put at last the deadly days to death
And fill the fields and fire the woods with thee
And seaward hollows where my feet would be
   When heaven shall hear the word that April saith
To change the cold heart of the weary time,
   To stir and soften all the time to tears,
      Tears joyfuller than mirth ;
As even to May's clear height the young days
   climb
   With feet not swifter than those fair first years
      Whose flowers revive not with thy flowers on
      earth.

VI

I would not bid thee, though I might, give back
   One good thing youth has given and borne away ;
   I crave not any comfort of the day
That is not, nor on time's retrodden track
Would turn to meet the white-robed hours or
   black
   That long since left me on their mortal way ;
Nor light nor love that has been, nor the breath
   That comes with morning from the sun to be
      And sets light hope on fire ;
No fruit, no flower thought once too fair for death,
   No flower nor hour once fallen from life's green
   tree,
      No leaf once plucked or once fulfilled desire.

VII

The morning song beneath the stars that fled
  With twilight through the moonless mountain air,
  While youth with burning lips and wreathless hair
Sang toward the sun that was to crown his head,
Rising ; the hopes that triumphed and fell dead,
  The sweet swift eyes and songs of hours that were ;
These may'st thou not give back for ever ; these,
  As at the sea's heart all her wrecks lie waste,
    Lie deeper than the sea ;
But flowers thou may'st, and winds, and hours of ease,
  And all its April to the world thou may'st
    Give back, and half my April back to me.

CHORIAMBICS

Love, what ailed thee to leave life that was made
    lovely, we thought, with love?
What sweet visions of sleep lured thee away, down
    from the light above?

What strange faces of dreams, voices that called,
    hands that were raised to wave,
Lured or led thee, alas, out of the sun, down to the
    sunless grave?

Ah, thy luminous eyes! once was their light fed with
    the fire of day;
Now their shadowy lids cover them close, hush them
    and hide away.

Ah, thy snow-coloured hands! once were they chains,
    mighty to bind me fast;
Now no blood in them burns, mindless of love, sense-
    less of passion past.

Ah, thy beautiful hair! so was it once braided for
    me, for me;
Now for death is it crowned, only for death, lover
    and lord of thee.

Sweet, the kisses of death set on thy lips, colder are
    they than mine ;
Colder surely than past kisses that love poured for
    thy lips as wine.

Lov'st thou death ? is his face fairer than love's,
    brighter to look upon ?
Seest thou light in his eyes, light by which love's
    pales and is overshone ?

Lo the roses of death, grey as the dust, chiller of leaf
    than snow !
Why let fall from thy hand love's that were thine,
    roses that loved thee so ?

Large red lilies of love, sceptral and tall, lovely for
    eyes to see ;
Thornless blossom of love, full of the sun, fruits that
    were reared for thee.

Now death's poppies alone circle thy hair, girdle thy
    breasts as white ;
Bloodless blossoms of death, leaves that have sprung
    never against the light.

Nay then, sleep if thou wilt ; love is content ; what
    should he do to weep ?
Sweet was love to thee once ; now in thine eyes
    sweeter than love is sleep.

AT PARTING

For a day and a night Love sang to us, played with
    us,
  Folded us round from the dark and the light ;
And our hearts were fulfilled of the music he made
    with us,
Made with our hearts and our lips while he stayed
    with us,
  Stayed in mid passage his pinions from flight
      For a day and a night.

From his foes that kept watch with his wings had he
    hidden us,
  Covered us close from the eyes that would smite,
From the feet that had tracked and the tongues that
    had chidden us
Sheltering in shade of the myrtles forbidden us
  Spirit and flesh growing one with delight
      For a day and a night.

But his wings will not rest and his feet will not stay
    for us :
  Morning is here in the joy of its might ;
With his breath has he sweetened a night and a day
    for us ;
Now let him pass, and the myrtles make way for us ;
  Love can but last in us here at his height
      For a day and a night.

A SONG IN SEASON

I

Thou whose beauty
Knows no duty
Due to love that moves thee never ;
Thou whose mercies
Are men's curses,
And thy smile a scourge for ever ;

II

Thou that givest
Death and livest
On the death of thy sweet giving ;
Thou that sparest
Not nor carest
Though thy scorn leave no love living ;

III

Thou whose rootless
Flower is fruitless
As the pride its heart encloses,
But thine eyes are
As May skies are,
And thy words like spoken roses ;

IV

Thou whose grace is
In men's faces
Fierce and wayward as thy will is ;
Thou whose peerless
Eyes are tearless,
And thy thoughts as cold sweet lilies ;

V

Thou that takest
Hearts and makest
Wrecks of loves to strew behind thee,
Whom the swallow
Sure should follow,
Finding summer where we find thee ;

VI

Thou that wakest
Hearts and breakest,
And thy broken hearts forgive thee,
That wilt make no
Pause and take no
Gift that love for love might give thee ;

VII

Thou that bindest
Eyes and blindest,
Serving worst who served thee longest ;
Thou that speakest,
And the weakest
Heart is his that was the strongest ;

VIII

Take in season
Thought with reason ;
Think what gifts are ours for giving ;
Hear what beauty
Owes of duty
To the love that keeps it living.

IX

Dust that covers
Long dead lovers
Song blows off with breath that brightens ;
At its flashes
Their white ashes
Burst in bloom that lives and lightens.

X

Had they bent not
Head or lent not
Ear to love and amorous duties,
Song had never
Saved for ever,
Love, the least of all their beauties.

XI

All the golden
Names of olden
Women yet by men's love cherished,
All our dearest
Thoughts hold nearest,
Had they loved not, all had perished.

XII

If no fruit is
Of thy beauties,
Tell me yet, since none may win them,
What and wherefore
Love should care for
Of all good things hidden in them?

XIII

Pain for profit
Comes but of it,
If the lips that lure their lover's
Hold no treasure
Past the measure
Of the lightest hour that hovers.

XIV

If they give not
Or forgive not
Gifts or thefts for grace or guerdon,
Love that misses
Fruit of kisses
Long will bear no thankless burden.

XV

If they care not
Though love were not,
If no breath of his burn through them,
Joy must borrow
Song from sorrow,
Fear teach hope the way to woo them.

XVI

Grief has measures
Soft as pleasure's,
Fear has moods that hope lies deep in,
Songs to sing him,
Dreams to bring him,
And a red-rose bed to sleep in.

XVII

Hope with fearless
Looks and tearless
Lies and laughs too near the thunder ;
Fear hath sweeter
Speech and meeter
For heart's love to hide him under.

XVIII

Joy by daytime
Fills his playtime
Full of songs loud mirth takes pride in ;
Night and morrow
Weave round sorrow
Thoughts as soft as sleep to hide in.

XIX

Graceless faces,
Loveless graces,
Are but motes in light that quicken,
Sands that run down
Ere the sundown,
Roseleaves dead ere autumn sicken.

xx

Fair and fruitless
Charms are bootless
Spells to ward off age's peril ;
Lips that give not
Love shall live not,
Eyes that meet not eyes are sterile.

xxi

But the beauty
Bound in duty
Fast to love that falls off never
Love shall cherish
Lest it perish,
And its root bears fruit for ever.

TWO LEADERS

βᾶτε δόμον, μεγάλοι φιλοτίμοι
Νυκτὸς παῖδες ἄπαιδες, ὑπ᾽ εὔφρονι πομπᾷ.

I

O GREAT and wise, clear-souled and high of heart,
  One the last flower of Catholic love, that grows
  Amid bare thorns their only thornless rose,
From the fierce juggling of the priests' loud mart
Yet alien, yet unspotted and apart
  From the blind hard foul rout whose shameless
    shows
  Mock the sweet heaven whose secret no man
    knows
With prayers and curses and the soothsayer's art ;
One like a storm-god of the northern foam
  Strong, wrought of rock that breasts and breaks
      the sea
    And thunders back its thunder, rhyme for rhyme
    Answering, as though to outroar the tides of
      time
  And bid the world's wave back—what song should
    be
Theirs that with praise would bring and sing you
    home ?

II

With all our hearts we praise you whom ye hate,
   High souls that hate us ; for our hopes are higher,
   And higher than yours the goal of our desire,
Though high your ends be as your hearts are great.
Your world of Gods and kings, of shrine and state,
   Was of the night when hope and fear stood nigher,
   Wherein men walked by light of stars and fire
Till man by day stood equal with his fate.
Honour not hate we give you, love not fear,
   Last prophets of past kind, who fill the dome
Of great dead Gods with wrath and wail, nor hear
   Time's word and man's : " Go honoured hence, go
      home,
Night's childless children ; here your hour is done ;
Pass with the stars, and leave us with the sun."

VICTOR HUGO IN 1877

"Dazzle mine eyes, or do I see three suns?"

ABOVE the spring-tide sundawn of the year,
    A sunlike star, not born of day or night,
    Filled the fair heaven of spring with heavenlier
        light,
Made of all ages orbed in one sole sphere
Whose light was as a Titan's smile or tear;
    Then rose a ray more flowerlike, starry white,
    Like a child's eye grown lovelier with delight,
Sweet as a child's heart-lightening laugh to hear;
And last a fire from heaven, a fiery rain
    As of God's wrath on the unclean cities, fell
    And lit the shuddering shades of half-seen hell
That shrank before it and were cloven in twain;
    A beacon fired by lightning, whence all time
    Sees red the bare black ruins of a crime.

CHILD'S SONG

WHAT is gold worth, say,
Worth for work or play,
Worth to keep or pay,
Hide or throw away,
    Hope about or fear?
What is love worth, pray?
    Worth a tear?

Golden on the mould
Lie the dead leaves rolled
Of the wet woods old,
Yellow leaves and cold,
    Woods without a dove;
Gold is worth but gold;
    Love's worth love.

TRIADS

I

I

THE word of the sun to the sky,
  The word of the wind to the sea,
    The word of the moon to the night,
        What may it be?

II

The sense to the flower of the fly,
  The sense of the bird to the tree,
    The sense to the cloud of the light,
        Who can tell me?

III

The song of the fields to the kye,
  The song of the lime to the bee,
    The song of the depth to the height,
        Who knows all three?

II

I

The message of April to May
  That May sends on into June
    And June gives out to July
        For birthday boon;

II

The delight of the dawn in the day,
  The delight of the day in the noon,
    The delight of a song in a sigh
                That breaks the tune ;

III

The secret of passing away,
  The cost of the change of the moon,
    None knows it with ear or with eye,
                But all will soon.

III

I

The live wave's love for the shore,
  The shore's for the wave as it dies,
    The love of the thunder-fire
                That sears the skies,

II

We shall know not though life wax hoar,
  Till all life, spent into sighs,
    Burn out as consumed with desire
                Of death's strange eyes ;

III

Till the secret be secret no more
  In the light of one hour as it flies,
    Be the hour as of suns that expire
                Or suns that rise.

FOUR SONGS OF FOUR SEASONS

I

WINTER IN NORTHUMBERLAND

I

OUTSIDE the garden
The wet skies harden ;
The gates are barred on
    The summer side :
" Shut out the flower-time,
Sunbeam and shower-time ;
Make way for our time,"
    Wild winds have cried.
Green once and cheery,
The woods, worn weary,
Sigh as the dreary
    Weak sun goes home :
A great wind grapples
The wave, and dapples
The dead green floor of the sea with foam.

II

Through fell and moorland,
And salt-sea foreland,
Our noisy norland
    Resounds and rings ;

Waste waves thereunder
Are blown in sunder,
And winds make thunder
  With cloudwide wings ;
Sea-drift makes dimmer
The beacon's glimmer ;
Nor sail nor swimmer
  Can try the tides ;
And snowdrifts thicken
Where, when leaves quicken,
Under the heather the sundew hides.

III

Green land and red land,
Moorside and headland,
Are white as dead land,
  Are all as one ;
Nor honied heather,
Nor bells to gather,
Fair with fair weather
  And faithful sun :
Fierce frost has eaten
All flowers that sweeten
The fells rain-beaten ;
  And winds their foes
Have made the snow's bed
Down in the rose-bed ;
Deep in the snow's bed bury the rose.

IV

Bury her deeper
Than any sleeper ;
Sweet dreams will keep her
  All day, all night ;

Though sleep benumb her
And time o'ercome her,
She dreams of summer,
   And takes delight,
Dreaming and sleeping
In love's good keeping,
While rain is weeping
   And no leaves cling;
Winds will come bringing her
Comfort, and singing her
Stories and songs and good news of the spring.

V

Draw the white curtain
Close, and be certain
She takes no hurt in
   Her soft low bed;
She feels no colder,
And grows not older,
Though snows enfold her
   From foot to head;
She turns not chilly
Like weed and lily
In marsh or hilly
   High watershed,
Or green soft island
In lakes of highland;
She sleeps awhile, and she is not dead.

VI

For all the hours,
Come sun, come showers,
Are friends of flowers,
   And fairies all;

I 2

When frost entrapped her,
They came and lapped her
In leaves, and wrapped her
    With shroud and pall ;
In red leaves wound her,
With dead leaves bound her
Dead brows, and round her
    A death-knell rang ;
Rang the death-bell for her,
Sang, " is it well for her,
Well, is it well with you, rose ? " they sang.

VII

O what and where is
The rose now, fairies,
So shrill the air is,
    So wild the sky ?
Poor last of roses,
Her worst of woes is
The noise she knows is
    The winter's cry ;
His hunting hollo
Has scared the swallow ;
Fain would she follow
    And fain would fly :
But wind unsettles
Her poor last petals ;
Had she but wings, and she would not die.

VIII

Come, as you love her,
Come close and cover
Her white face over,
    And forth again

Ere sunset glances
On foam that dances,
Through lowering lances
  Of bright white rain ;
And make your playtime
Of winter's daytime,
As if the Maytime
  Were here to sing ;
As if the snowballs
Were soft like blowballs,
Blown in a mist from the stalk in the spring.

IX

Each reed that grows in
Our stream is frozen,
The fields it flows in
  Are hard and black ;
The water-fairy
Waits wise and wary
Till time shall vary
  And thaws come back.
"O sister, water,"
The wind besought her,
"O twin-born daughter
  Of spring with me,
Stay with me, play with me,
Take the warm way with me,
Straight for the summer and oversea."

X

But winds will vary,
And wise and wary
The patient fairy
  Of water waits ;

All shrunk and wizen,
In iron prison,
Till spring re-risen
  Unbar the gates ;
Till, as with clamour
Of axe and hammer,
Chained streams that stammer
  And struggle in straits
Burst bonds that shiver,
And thaws deliver
The roaring river in stormy spates.

XI

In fierce March weather
White waves break tether,
And whirled together
  At either hand,
Like weeds uplifted,
The tree-trunks rifted
In spars are drifted,
  Like foam or sand,
Past swamp and sallow
And reed-beds callow,
Through pool and shallow,
  To wind and lee,
Till, no more tongue-tied,
Full flood and young tide
Roar down the rapids and storm the sea.

XII

As men's cheeks faded
On shores invaded,
When shorewards waded
  The lords of fight ;

When churl and craven
Saw hard on haven
The wide-winged raven
    At mainmast height ;
When monks affrighted
To windward sighted
The birds full-flighted
    Of swift sea-kings ;
So earth turns paler
When Storm the sailor
Steers in with a roar in the race of his wings.

XIII

O strong sea-sailor,
Whose cheek turns paler
For wind or hail or
    For fear of thee ?
O far sea-farer,
O thunder-bearer,
Thy songs are rarer
    Than soft songs be.
O fleet-foot stranger,
O north-sea ranger
Through days of danger
    And ways of fear,
Blow thy horn here for us,
Blow the sky clear for us,
Send us the song of the sea to hear.

XIV

Roll the strong stream of it
Up, till the scream of it
Wake from a dream of it
    Children that sleep,

Seamen that fare for them
Forth, with a prayer for them ;
Shall not God care for them,
    Angels not keep ?
Spare not the surges
Thy stormy scourges ;
Spare us the dirges
    Of wives that weep.
Turn back the waves for us :
Dig no fresh graves for us,
Wind, in the manifold gulfs of the deep.

XV

O stout north-easter,
Sea-king, land-waster,
For all thine haste, or
    Thy stormy skill,
Yet hadst thou never,
For all endeavour,
Strength to dissever
    Or strength to spill,
Save of his giving
Who gave our living,
Whose hands are weaving
    What ours fulfil ;
Whose feet tread under
The storms and thunder ;
Who made our wonder to work his will.

XVI

His years and hours,
His world's blind powers,
His stars and flowers,
    His nights and days,

Sea-tide and river,
And waves that shiver,
Praise God, the giver
　　Of tongues to praise.
Winds in their blowing,
And fruits in growing;
Time in its going,
　　While time shall be;
In death and living,
With one thanksgiving,
Praise him whose hand is the strength of the
　　sea.

II

SPRING IN TUSCANY

ROSE-RED lilies that bloom on the banner ;
  Rose-cheeked gardens that revel in spring ;
    Rose-mouthed acacias that laugh as they
      climb,
Like plumes for a queen's hand fashioned to fan her
  With wind more soft than a wild dove's wing,
    What do they sing in the spring of their time ?

If this be the rose that the world hears singing,
  Soft in the soft night, loud in the day,
    Songs for the fire-flies to dance as they hear ;
If that be the song of the nightingale, springing
  Forth in the form of a rose in May,
    What do they say of the way of the year ?

What of the way of the world gone Maying,
  What of the work of the buds in the bowers,
    What of the will of the wind on the wall,
Fluttering the wall-flowers, sighing and playing,
  Shrinking again as a bird that cowers,
    Thinking of hours when the flowers have to
      fall ?

Out of the throats of the loud birds showering,
  Out of the folds where the flag-lilies leap,
    Out of the mouths of the roses stirred,

Out of the herbs on the walls reflowering,
　　Out of the heights where the sheer snows sleep,
　　　　Out of the deep and the steep, one word.

One from the lips of the lily-flames leaping,
　　The glad red lilies that burn in our sight,
　　　　The great live lilies for standard and crown ;
One from the steeps where the pines stand sleeping,
　　One from the deep land, one from the height,
　　　　One from the light and the might of the town.

The lowlands laugh with delight of the highlands,
　　Whence May winds feed them with balm and
　　　　breath
　　　　From hills that beheld in the years behind
A shape as of one from the blest souls' islands,
　　Made fair by a soul too fair for death,
　　　　With eyes on the light that should smite them
　　　　blind.

Vallombrosa remotely remembers,
　　Perchance, what still to us seems so near
　　　　That time not darkens it, change not mars,
The foot that she knew when her leaves were
　　September's,
　　The face lift up to the star-blind seer,
　　　　That saw from his prison arisen his stars.

And Pisa broods on her dead, not mourning,
　　For love of her loveliness given them in fee ;
　　　　And Prato gleams with the glad monk's gift
Whose hand was there as the hand of morning ;
　　And Siena, set in the sand's red sea,
　　　　Lifts loftier her head than the red sand's drift.

And far to the fair south-westward lightens,
  Girdled and sandalled and plumed with flowers,
    At sunset over the love-lit lands,
The hill-side's crown where the wild hill brightens,
  Saint Fina's town of the Beautiful Towers,
    Hailing the sun with a hundred hands.

Land of us all that have loved thee dearliest,
  Mother of men that were lords of man,
      Whose name in the world's heart works as a
        spell,
My last song's light, and the star of mine earliest,
  As we turn from thee, sweet, who wast ours for a
    span,
      Fare well we may not who say farewell.

III

SUMMER IN AUVERGNE

THE sundawn fills the land
Full as a feaster's hand
Fills full with bloom of bland
    Bright wine his cup ;
Flows full to flood that fills
From the arch of air it thrills
Those rust-red iron hills
    With morning up.

Dawn, as a panther springs,
With fierce and fire-fledged wings
Leaps on the land that rings
    From her bright feet
Through all its lava-black
Cones that cast answer back
And cliffs of footless track
    Where thunders meet.

The light speaks wide and loud
From deeps blown clean of cloud
As though day's heart were proud
    And heaven's were glad ;
The towers brown-striped and grey
Take fire from heaven of day
As though the prayers they pray
    Their answers had.

Higher in these high first hours
Wax all the keen church towers,
And higher all hearts of ours
    Than the old hills' crown,
Higher than the pillared height
Of that strange cliff-side bright
With basalt towers whose might
    Strong time bows down.

And the old fierce ruin there
Of the old wild princes' lair
Whose blood in mine hath share
    Gapes gaunt and great
Toward heaven that long ago
Watched all the wan land's woe
Whereon the wind would blow
    Of their bleak hate.

Dead are those deeds ; but yet
Their memory seems to fret
Lands that might else forget
    That old world's brand ;
Dead all their sins and days ;
Yet in this red clime's rays
Some fiery memory stays
    That sears their land.

IV

AUTUMN IN CORNWALL

THE year lies fallen and faded
On cliffs by clouds invaded,
With tongues of storms upbraided,
   With wrath of waves bedinned ;
And inland, wild with warning,
As in deaf ears or scorning,
The clarion even and morning
   Rings of the south-west wind.

The wild bents wane and wither
In blasts whose breath bows hither
Their grey-grown heads and thither,
   Unblest of rain or sun ;
The pale fierce heavens are crowded
With shapes like dreams beclouded,
As though the old year enshrouded
   Lay, long ere life were done.

Full-charged with oldworld wonders,
From dusk Tintagel thunders
A note that smites and sunders
   The hard frore fields of air ;
A trumpet stormier-sounded
Than once from lists rebounded
When strong men sense-confounded
   Fell thick in tourney there.

From scarce a duskier dwelling
Such notes of wail rose welling
Through the outer darkness, telling
    In the awful singer's ears
What souls the darkness covers,
What love-lost souls of lovers,
Whose cry still hangs and hovers
    In each man's born that hears.

For there by Hector's brother
And yet some thousand other
He that had grief to mother
    Passed pale from Dante's sight ;
With one fast linked as fearless,
Perchance, there only tearless ;
Iseult and Tristram, peerless
    And perfect queen and knight.

A shrill-winged sound comes flying
North, as of wild souls crying
The cry of things undying,
    That know what life must be ;
Or as the old year's heart, stricken
Too sore for hope to quicken
By thoughts like thorns that thicken,
    Broke, breaking with the sea.

THE WHITE CZAR

[In an English magazine of 1877 there appeared a version of some insolent lines addressed by "A Russian Poet to the Empress of India." To these the first of the two following sonnets was designed to serve by way of counterblast. The writer will scarcely be suspected of royalism or imperialism ; but it seemed to him that an insult levelled by Muscovite lips at the ruler of England might perhaps be less unfitly than unofficially resented by an Englishman who was also a republican.]

I

GEHAZI by the hue that chills thy cheek
  And Pilate by the hue that sears thine hand
  Whence all earth's waters cannot wash the brand
That signs thy soul a manslayer's though thou speak
All Christ, with lips most murderous and most meek—
  Thou set thy foot where England's used to stand !
  Thou reach thy rod forth over Indian land !
Slave of the slaves that call thee lord, and weak
As their foul tongues who praise thee ! son of them
Whose presence put the snows and stars to shame
  In centuries dead and damned that reek below
Curse-consecrated, crowned with crime and flame,
  To them that bare thee like them shalt thou go
  Forth of man's life—a leper white as snow.

II

Call for clear water, wash thine hands, be clean,
　　Cry, *What is truth?* O Pilate ; thou shalt know
　　Haply too soon, and gnash thy teeth for woe
Ere the outer darkness take thee round unseen
That hides the red ghosts of thy race obscene
　　Bound nine times round with hell's most dolorous
　　　　flow,
　　And in its pools thy crownless head lie low
By his of Spain who dared an English queen
With half a world to hearten him for fight,
Till the wind gave his warriors and their might
　　To shipwreck and the corpse-encumbered sea.
But thou, take heed, ere yet thy lips wax white,
　　Lest as it was with Philip so it be,
　　O white of name and red of hand, with thee.

RIZPAH

How many sons, how many generations,
  For how long years hast thou bewept, and known
  Nor end of torment nor surcease of moan,
Rachel or Rizpah, wofullest of nations,
Crowned with the crowning sign of desolations,
  And couldst not even scare off with hand or groan
  Those carrion birds devouring bone by bone
The children of thy thousand tribulations?
Thou wast our warrior once; thy sons long dead
Against a foe less foul than this made head,
  Poland, in years that sound and shine afar;
Ere the east beheld in thy bright sword-blade's stead
  The rotten corpse-light of the Russian star
  That lights towards hell his bondslaves and their
    Czar.

TO LOUIS KOSSUTH

1877

Light of our fathers' eyes, and in our own
   Star of the unsetting sunset! for thy name,
   That on the front of noon was as a flame
In the great year nigh thirty years agone
When all the heavens of Europe shook and shone
   With stormy wind and lightning, keeps its fame
   And bears its witness all day through the same;
Not for past days and great deeds past alone,
Kossuth, we praise thee as our Landor praised,
But that now too we know thy voice upraised,
Thy voice, the trumpet of the truth of God,
   Thine hand, the thunder-bearer's, raised to smite
As with heaven's lightning for a sword and rod
   Men's heads abased before the Muscovite.

TRANSLATIONS FROM THE FRENCH OF VILLON

THE COMPLAINT OF THE FAIR ARMOURESS

I

MESEEMETH I heard cry and groan
 That sweet who was the armourer's maid ;
For her young years she made sore moan,
 And right upon this wise she said ;
 " Ah fierce old age with foul bald head,
To spoil fair things thou art over fain ;
 Who holdeth me ? who ? would God I were
  dead !
Would God I were well dead and slain !

II

" Lo, thou hast broken the sweet yoke
 That my high beauty held above
All priests and clerks and merchant-folk ;
 There was not one but for my love
 Would give me gold and gold enough,
Though sorrow his very heart had riven,
 To win from me such wage thereof
As now no thief would take if given.

iii

"I was right chary of the same,
  God wot it was my great folly,
For love of one sly knave of them,
  Good store of that same sweet had he ;
  For all my subtle wiles, perdie,
God wot I loved him well enow ;
  Right evilly he handled me,
But he loved well my gold, I trow.

iv

"Though I gat bruises green and black,
  I loved him never the less a jot ;
Though he bound burdens on my back,
  If he said ' Kiss me and heed it not '
  Right little pain I felt, God wot,
When that foul thief's mouth, found so sweet,
  Kissed me—Much good thereof I got !
I keep the sin and the shame of it.

v

"And he died thirty year agone.
  I am old now, no sweet thing to see ;
By God, though, when I think thereon,
  And of that good glad time, woe's me,
  And stare upon my changed body
Stark naked, that has been so sweet,
  Lean, wizen, like a small dry tree,
I am nigh mad with the pain of it.

VI

" Where is my faultless forehead's white,
    The lifted eyebrows, soft gold hair,
Eyes wide apart and keen of sight,
    With subtle skill in the amorous air ;
    The straight nose, great nor small, but fair,
The small carved ears of shapeliest growth,
    Chin dimpling, colour good to wear,
And sweet red splendid kissing mouth ?

VII

" The shapely slender shoulders small,
    Long arms, hands wrought in glorious wise,
Round little breasts, the hips withal
    High, full of flesh, not scant of size,
    Fit for all amorous masteries ;

*** ***** *****, *** *** ****** **** ***
    ****** ***** ** **** ***** ******
** * ***** ****** ** **** ***** ?

VIII

" A writhled forehead, hair gone grey,
    Fallen eyebrows, eyes gone blind and red,
Their laughs and looks all fled away,
    Yea, all that smote men's hearts are fled ;
    The bowed nose, fallen from goodlihead ;
Foul flapping ears like water-flags ;
    Peaked chin, and cheeks all waste and dead,
And lips that are two skinny rags :

IX

"Thus endeth all the beauty of us.
    The arms made short, the hands made lean,
The shoulders bowed and ruinous,
    The breasts, alack ! all fallen in ;
    The flanks too, like the breasts, grown thin ;
** *** *** ***** ***** , *** ** ** !
    For the lank thighs, no thighs but skin,
They are specked with spots like sausage-meat.

X

"So we make moan for the old sweet days,
    Poor old light women, two or three
Squatting above the straw-fire's blaze,
    The bosom crushed against the knee,
    Like faggots on a heap we be,
Round fires soon lit, soon quenched and done ;
    And we were once so sweet, even we !
Thus fareth many and many an one."

A DOUBLE BALLAD OF GOOD COUNSEL

Now take your fill of love and glee,
    And after balls and banquets hie ;
In the end ye'll get no good for fee,
    But just heads broken by and by ;
    Light loves make beasts of men that sigh ;
They changed the faith of Solomon,
    And left not Samson lights to spy ;
Good luck has he that deals with none !

Sweet Orpheus, lord of minstrelsy,
    For this with flute and pipe came nigh
The danger of the dog's heads three
    That ravening at hell's door doth lie ;
    Fain was Narcissus, fair and shy,
For love's love lightly lost and won,
    In a deep well to drown and die ;
Good luck has he that deals with none !

Sardana, flower of chivalry,
    Who conquered Crete with horn and cry,
For this was fain a maid to be
    And learn with girls the thread to ply ;
    King David, wise in prophecy,
Forgot the fear of God for one
    Seen washing either shapely thigh ;
Good luck has he that deals with none !

BALLAD OF THE LORDS OF OLD TIME

(AFTER THE FORMER ARGUMENT)

WHAT more?   Where is the third Calixt,
    Last of that name now dead and gone,
Who held four years the Papalist?
        Alphonso king of Aragon,
        The gracious lord, duke of Bourbon,
And Arthur, duke of old Britaine?
        And Charles the Seventh, that worthy one?
Even with the good knight Charlemain.

The Scot too, king of mount and mist,
    With half his face vermilion,
Men tell us, like an amethyst
        From brow to chin that blazed and shone;
        The Cypriote king of old renown,
Alas! and that good king of Spain,
        Whose name I cannot think upon?
Even with the good knight Charlemain.

No more to say of them I list;
    'Tis all but vain, all dead and done:
For death may no man born resist,
        Nor make appeal when death comes on.
        I make yet one more question;
Where's Lancelot, king of far Bohain?
        Where's he whose grandson called him son?
Even with the good knight Charlemain.

Where is Guesclin, the good Breton?
    The lord of the eastern mountain-chain,
And the good late duke of Alençon?
    Even with the good knight Charlemain.

BALLAD OF THE WOMEN OF PARIS

ALBEIT the Venice girls get praise
    For their sweet speech and tender air,
And though the old women have wise ways
    Of chaffering for amorous ware,
    Yet at my peril dare I swear,
Search Rome, where God's grace mainly tarries,
    Florence and Savoy, everywhere,
There's no good girl's lip out of Paris.

The Naples women, as folk prattle,
    Are sweetly spoken and subtle enough :
German girls are good at tattle,
    And Prussians make their boast thereof ;
    Take Egypt for the next remove,
Or that waste land the Tartar harries,
    Spain or Greece, for the matter of love,
There's no good girl's lip out of Paris.

Breton and Swiss know nought of the matter,
    Gascony girls or girls of Toulouse ;
Two fishwives here with a half-hour's chatter
    Would shut them up by threes and twos ;
    Calais, Lorraine, and all their crews,
(Names enow the mad song marries)
    England and Picardy, search them and choose,
There's no good girl's lip out of Paris.

Prince, give praise to our French ladies
  For the sweet sound their speaking carries ;
'Twixt Rome and Cadiz many a maid is,
  But no good girl's lip out of Paris.

BALLAD WRITTEN FOR A BRIDEGROOM

WHICH VILLON GAVE TO A GENTLEMAN NEWLY MARRIED TO
SEND TO HIS WIFE WHOM HE HAD WON WITH THE SWORD

At daybreak, when the falcon claps his wings,
  No whit for grief, but noble heart and high,
With loud glad noise he stirs himself and springs,
  And takes his meat and toward his lure draws
      nigh ;
  Such good I wish you !   Yea, and heartily
I am fired with hope of true love's meed to get ;
  Know that Love writes it in his book ; for why,
This is the end for which we twain are met.

Mine own heart's lady with no gainsayings
  You shall be always wholly till I die ;
And in my right against all bitter things
  Sweet laurel with fresh rose its force shall try ;
  Seeing reason wills not that I cast love by
(Nor here with reason shall I chide or fret)
  Nor cease to serve, but serve more constantly ;
This is the end for which we twain are met.

And, which is more, when grief about me clings
  Through Fortune's fit or fume of jealousy,
Your sweet kind eye beats down her threatenings
  As wind doth smoke ; such power sits in your eye.

Thus in your field my seed of harvestry
Thrives, for the fruit is like me that I set ;
   God bids me tend it with good husbandry ;
This is the end for which we twain are met.

Princess, give ear to this my summary ;
   That heart of mine your heart's love should forget
Shall never be : like trust in you put I :
   This is the end for which we twain are met.

BALLAD AGAINST THE ENEMIES OF FRANCE

MAY he fall in with beasts that scatter fire,
 Like Jason, when he sought the fleece of gold,
Or change from man to beast three years entire,
 As King Nebuchadnezzar did of old ;
Or else have times as shameful and as bad
As Trojan folk for ravished Helen had ;
Or gulfed with Proserpine and Tantalus
Let hell's deep fen devour him dolorous,
 With worse to bear than Job's worst sufferance,
Bound in his prison-maze with Dædalus,
 Who could wish evil to the state of France !

May he four months, like bitterns in the mire,
 Howl with head downmost in the lake-springs
  cold,
Or to bear harness like strong bulls for hire
 To the Great Turk for money down be sold ;
Or thirty years like Magdalen live sad,
With neither wool nor web of linen clad ;
Drown like Narciss', or swing down pendulous
Like Absalom with locks luxurious,
 Or liker Judas fallen to reprobance ;
Or find such death as Simon sorcerous,
 Who could wish evil to the state of France !

May the old times come of fierce Octavian's ire,
 And in his belly molten coin be told ;
May he like Victor in the mill expire,
 Crushed between moving millstones on him rolled,

Or in deep sea drenched breathless, more adrad
Than in the whale's bulk Jonas, when God bade :
From Phœbus' light, from Juno's treasure-house
Driven, and from joys of Venus amorous,
    And cursed of God most high to the utterance,
As was the Syrian king Antiochus,
    Who could wish evil to the state of France !

Prince, may the bright-winged brood of Æolus
To sea-king Glaucus' wild wood cavernous
    Bear him bereft of peace and hope's least glance,
For worthless is he to get good of us,
    Who could wish evil to the state of France.

THE DISPUTE OF THE HEART AND BODY OF
FRANÇOIS VILLON

Who is this I hear?—Lo, this is I, thine heart,
 That holds on merely now by a slender string.
Strength fails me, shape and sense are rent apart,
 The blood in me is turned to a bitter thing,
 Seeing thee skulk here like a dog shivering.—
Yea, and for what?—For that thy sense found
  sweet.—
What irks it thee?—I feel the sting of it.—
 Leave me at peace.—Why?—Nay now, leave me
  at peace;
I will repent when I grow ripe in wit.—
 I say no more.—I care not though thou cease.—

What art thou, trow?—A man worth praise, perfay.—
 This is thy thirtieth year of wayfaring.—
'Tis a mule's age.—Art thou a boy still?—Nay.—
 Is it hot lust that spurs thee with its sting,
 Grasping thy throat? Know'st thou not any-
  thing?—
Yea, black and white, when milk is specked with
  flies,
I can make out.—No more?—Nay, in no wise.
 Shall I begin again the count of these?—
Thou art undone.—I will make shift to rise.—
 I say no more.—I care not though thou cease.—

I have the sorrow of it, and thou the smart.
  Wert thou a poor mad fool or weak of wit,
Then might'st thou plead this pretext with thine
      heart ;
  But if thou know not good from evil a whit,
  Either thy head is hard as stone to hit,
Or shame, not honour, gives thee most content.
What canst thou answer to this argument ?—
  When I am dead I shall be well at ease.—
God ! what good hope !—Thou art over eloquent.—
  I say no more.—I care not though thou cease.—

Whence is this ill ?—From sorrow and not from sin.
  When Saturn packed my wallet up for me
I well believe he put these ills therein.—
  Fool, wilt thou make thy servant lord of thee ?
  Hear now the wise king's counsel ; thus saith he :
All power upon the stars a wise man hath ;
There is no planet that shall do him scathe.—
  Nay, as they made me I grow and I decrease.—
What say'st thou ?—Truly this is all my faith.—
  I say no more.—I care not though thou cease.—

Wouldst thou live still ?—God help me that I
      may !—
Then thou must—What ? turn penitent and pray ?—
Read always—What ?—Grave words and good to
      say ;
  Leave off the ways of fools, lest they displease.—
Good ; I will do it.—Wilt thou remember ?—Yea.—
Abide not till there come an evil day.
  I say no more.—I care not though thou cease.

EPISTLE IN FORM OF A BALLAD TO HIS FRIENDS

HAVE pity, pity, friends, have pity on me,
   Thus much at least, may it please you, of your
      grace !
I lie not under hazel or hawthorn-tree
   Down in this dungeon ditch, mine exile's place
   By leave of God and fortune's foul disgrace.
Girls, lovers, glad young folk and newly wed,
Jumpers and jugglers, tumbling heel o'er head,
   Swift as a dart, and sharp as needle-ware,
Throats clear as bells that ring the kine to shed,
   Your poor old friend, what, will you leave him
      there ?

Singers that sing at pleasure, lawlessly,
   Light, laughing, gay of word and deed, that race
And run like folk light-witted as ye be
   And have in hand nor current coin nor base,
   Ye wait too long, for now he's dying apace.
Rhymers of lays and roundels sung and read,
Ye'll brew him broth too late when he lies dead.
   Nor wind nor lightning, sunbeam nor fresh air,
May pierce the thick wall's bound where lies his
      bed ;
   Your poor old friend, what, will you leave him
      there ?

O noble folk from tithes and taxes free,
   Come and behold him in this piteous case,
Ye that nor king nor emperor holds in fee,
   But only God in heaven ; behold his face
   Who needs must fast, Sundays and holidays,
Which makes his teeth like rakes ; and when he hath
      fed
With never a cake for banquet but dry bread,
   Must drench his bowels with much cold watery
      fare,
With board nor stool, but low on earth instead ;
   Your poor old friend, what, will you leave him
      there ?

Princes afore-named, old and young foresaid,
Get me the king's seal and my pardon sped,
   And hoist me in some basket up with care :
So swine will help each other ill bested,
For where one squeaks they run in heaps ahead.
   Your poor old friend, what, will you leave him
         there ?

THE EPITAPH IN FORM OF A BALLAD

WHICH VILLON MADE FOR HIMSELF AND HIS COMRADES,
EXPECTING TO BE HANGED ALONG WITH THEM

MEN, brother men, that after us yet live,
    Let not your hearts too hard against us be ;
For if some pity of us poor men ye give,
    The sooner God shall take of you pity.
    Here are we five or six strung up, you see,
And here the flesh that all too well we fed
Bit by bit eaten and rotten, rent and shred,
    And we the bones grow dust and ash withal ;
Let no man laugh at us discomforted,
    But pray to God that he forgive us all.

If we call on you, brothers, to forgive,
    Ye should not hold our prayer in scorn, though we
Were slain by law ; ye know that all alive
    Have not wit alway to walk righteously ;
    Make therefore intercession heartily
With him that of a virgin's womb was bred,
That his grace be not as a dry well-head
    For us, nor let hell's thunder on us fall ;
We are dead, let no man harry or vex us dead,
    But pray to God that he forgive us all.

The rain has washed and laundered us all five,
    And the sun dried and blackened ; yea, perdie,
Ravens and pies with beaks that rend and rive
    Have dug our eyes out, and plucked off for fee
    Our beards and eyebrows ; never are we free,

Not once, to rest ; but here and there still sped,
Drive at its wild will by the wind's change led,
  More pecked of birds than fruits on garden-wall ;
Men, for God's love, let no gibe here be said,
  But pray to God that he forgive us all.

Prince Jesus, that of all art lord and head,
Keep us, that hell be not our bitter bed ;
  We have nought to do in such a master's hall.
Be not ye therefore of our fellowhead,
  But pray to God that he forgive us all.

FROM VICTOR HUGO

TAKE heed of this small child of earth;
 He is great: he hath in him God most high.
Children before their fleshly birth
 Are lights alive in the blue sky.

In our light bitter world of wrong
 They come; God gives us them awhile.
His speech is in their stammering tongue,
 And his forgiveness in their smile.

Their sweet light rests upon our eyes.
 Alas! their right to joy is plain.
If they are hungry, Paradise
 Weeps, and, if cold, Heaven thrills with pain.

The want that saps their sinless flower
 Speaks judgment on sin's ministers.
Man holds an angel in his power.
 Ah! deep in Heaven what thunder stirs,

When God seeks out these tender things
 Whom in the shadow where we sleep
He sends us clothed about with wings,
 And finds them ragged babes that weep!

NOCTURNE

La nuit écoute et se penche sur l'onde
Pour y cueillir rien qu'un souffle d'amour ;
Pas de lueur, pas de musique au monde,
Pas de sommeil pour moi ni de séjour.
O mère, ô Nuit, de ta source profonde
Verse-nous, verse enfin l'oubli du jour.

Verse l'oubli de l'angoisse et du jour ;
Chante ; ton chant assoupit l'âme et l'onde :
Fais de ton sein pour mon âme un séjour,
Elle est bien lasse, ô mère, de ce monde,
Où le baiser ne veut pas dire amour,
Où l'âme aimée est moins que toi profonde.

Car toute chose aimée est moins profonde,
O Nuit, que toi, fille et mère du jour ;
Toi dont l'attente est le répit du monde,
Toi dont le souffle est plein de mots d'amour,
Toi dont l'haleine enfle et réprime l'onde,
Toi dont l'ombre a tout le ciel pour séjour.

La misère humble et lasse, sans séjour,
S'abrite et dort sous ton aile profonde ;
Tu fais à tous l'aumône de l'amour :
Toutes les soifs viennent boire à ton onde,
Tout ce qui pleure et se dérobe au jour,
Toutes les faims et tous les maux du monde.

Moi seul je veille et ne vois dans ce monde
Que ma douleur qui n'ait point de séjour
Où s'abriter sur ta rive profonde
Et s'endormir sous tes yeux loin du jour ;
Je vais toujours cherchant au bord de l'onde
Le sang du beau pied blessé de l'amour.

La mer est sombre où tu naquis, amour,
Pleine des pleurs et des sanglots du monde ;
On ne voit plus le gouffre où naît le jour
Luire et frémir sous ta lueur profonde ;
Mais dans les cœurs d'homme où tu fais séjour
La douleur monte et baisse comme une onde.

ENVOI

Fille de l'onde et mère de l'amour,
Du haut séjour plein de ta paix profonde
Sur ce bas monde épands un peu de jour.

THÉOPHILE GAUTIER

Pour mettre une couronne au front d'une chanson,
Il semblait qu'en passant son pied semât des roses,
Et que sa main cueillît comme des fleurs écloses
Les étoiles au fond du ciel en floraison.

Sa parole de marbre et d'or avait le son
Des clairons de l'été chassant les jours moroses ;
Comme en Thrace Apollon banni des grands cieux
    roses,
Il regardait du cœur l'Olympe, sa maison.

Le soleil fut pour lui le soleil du vieux monde,
Et son œil recherchait dans les flots embrasés
Le sillon immortel d'où s'élança sur l'onde
Vénus, que la mer molle enivrait de baisers :
Enfin, dieu ressaisi de sa splendeur première,
Il trône, et son sépulcre est bâti de lumière.

ODE

(LE TOMBEAU DE THÉOPHILE GAUTIER)

QUELLE fleur, ô Mort, quel joyau, quel chant,
Quel vent, quel rayon de soleil couchant,
Sur ton front penché, sur ta main avide,
Sur l'âpre pâleur de ta lèvre aride,
 Vibre encore et luit ?
Ton sein est sans lait, ton oreille est vide,
 Ton œil plein de nuit.

Ta bouche est sans souffle et ton front sans ride ;
Mais l'éclair voilé d'une flamme humide,
Flamme éclose au cœur d'un ciel pluvieux,
Rallume ta lèvre et remplit tes yeux
 De lueurs d'opale ;
Ta bouche est vermeille et ton front joyeux,
 O toi qui fus pâle.

Comme aux jours divins la mère des dieux,
Reine au sein fécond, au corps radieux,
Tu surgis au bord de la tombe amère ;
Tu nous apparais, ô Mort, vierge et mère,
 Effroi des humains,
Le divin laurier sur la tête altière
 Et la lyre aux mains.

Nous reconnaissons, courbés vers la terre,
Que c'est la splendeur de ta face austère
Qui dore la nuit de nos longs malheurs ;
Que la vie ailée aux mille couleurs,
        Dont tu n'es que l'âme,
Refait par tes mains les prés et les fleurs,
        La rose et la femme.

Lune constante ! astre ami des douleurs
Qui luis à travers la brume des pleurs !
Quelle flamme au fond de ta clarté molle
Éclate et rougit, nouvelle auréole,
        Ton doux front voilé ?
Quelle étoile, ouvrant ses ailes, s'envole
        Du ciel étoilé ?

Pleurant ce rayon de jour qu'on lui vole,
L'homme exècre en vain la Mort triste et folle ;
Mais l'astre qui fut à nos yeux si beau,
Là-haut, loin d'ici, dans un ciel nouveau
        Plein d'autres étoiles,
Se lève, et pour lui la nuit du tombeau
        Entr'ouvre ses voiles.

L'âme est dans le corps comme un jeune oiseau
Dont l'aile s'agite au bord du berceau ;
La mort, déliant cette aile inquiète,
Quand nous écoutons la bouche muette
        Qui nous dit adieu,
Fait de l'homme infime et sombre un poëte,
        Du poëte un dieu.

IN OBITUM THEOPHILI POETÆ

O LUX Pieridum et laurigeri deliciæ dei,
Vox leni Zephyro lenior, ut veris amans novi
Tollit floridulis implicitum primitiis caput,
Ten' ergo abripuit non rediturum, ut redeunt novo
Flores vere novi, te quoque mors irrevocabilem?
Cur vatem neque te Musa parens, te neque Gratiæ,
Nec servare sibi te potuit fidum animi Venus?
Quæ nunc ipsa magis vel puero te Cinyreïo,
Te desiderium et flebilibus lumen amoribus,
Amissum queritur, sanguineis fusa comam genis.
Tantis tu lacrymis digne, comes dulcis Apollini,
Carum nomen eris dîs superis atque sodalibus
Nobis, quîs eadem quæ tibi vivo patuit via
Non æquis patet, at te sequimur passibus haud tuis,
At mæsto cinerem carmine non illacrymabilem
Tristesque exuvias floribus ac fletibus integris
Unà contegimus, nec citharâ nec sine tibiâ,
Votoque unanimæ vocis Ave dicimus et Vale.

AD CATULLUM

CATULLE frater, ut velim comes tibi
Remota per vireta, per cavum nemus
Sacrumque Ditis haud inhospiti specus,
Pedem referre, trans aquam Stygis ducem
Secutus unum et unicum, Catulle, te,
Ut ora vatis optimi reviserem,
Tui meique vatis ora, quem scio
Venustiorem adîsse vel tuo lacum,
Benigniora semper arva vel tuis,
Ubi serenus accipit suos deus,
Tegitque myrtus implicata laureâ,
Manuque mulcet halituque consecrat
Fovetque blanda mors amabili sinu,
Et ore fama fervido colit viros
Alitque qualis unus ille par tibi
Britannus unicusque in orbe præstitit
Amicus ille noster, ille ceteris
Poeta major, omnibusque floribus
Priore Landor inclytum rosâ caput
Revinxit extulitque, quam tuâ manu
Recepit ac refovit integram suâ.

DEDICATION

1878

SOME nine years gone, as we dwelt together
In the sweet hushed heat of the south French
weather
 Ere autumn fell on the vine-tressed hills
Or the season had shed one rose-red feather,

Friend, whose fame is a flame that fills
All eyes it lightens and hearts it thrills
 With joy to be born of the blood which bred
From a land that the grey sea girds and chills

The heart and spirit and hand and head
Whose might is as light on a dark day shed,
 On a day now dark as a land's decline
Where all the peers of your praise are dead,

In a land and season of corn and vine
I pledged you a health from a beaker of mine
 But halfway filled to the lip's edge yet
With hope for honey and song for wine.

Nine years have risen and eight years set
Since there by the wellspring our hands on it met :
    And the pledge of my songs that were then to be,
I could wonder not, friend, though a friend should
      forget.

For life's helm rocks to the windward and lee,
And time is as wind, and as waves are we ;
    And song is as foam that the sea-winds fret,
Though the thought at its heart should be deep as
      the sea.

POEMS AND BALLADS

THIRD SERIES

MARCH: AN ODE

1887

I

ERE frost-flower and snow-blossom faded and fell,
and the splendour of winter had passed out of
sight,
The ways of the woodlands were fairer and stranger
than dreams that fulfil us in sleep with delight ;
The breath of the mouths of the winds had hardened
on tree-tops and branches that glittered and
swayed
Such wonders and glories of blossomlike snow or of
frost that outlightens all flowers till it fade
That the sea was not lovelier than here was the land,
nor the night than the day, nor the day than the
night,
Nor the winter sublimer with storm than the spring :
such mirth had the madness and might in thee
made,
March, master of winds, bright minstrel and marshal
of storms that enkindle the season they smite.

II

And now that the rage of thy rapture is satiate with
    revel and ravin and spoil of the snow,
And the branches it brightened are broken, and
    shattered the tree-tops that only thy wrath could
    lay low,
How should not thy lovers rejoice in thee, leader and
    lord of the year that exults to be born
So strong in thy strength and so glad of thy glad-
    ness whose laughter puts winter and sorrow to
    scorn?
Thou hast shaken the snows from thy wings, and the
    frost on thy forehead is molten: thy lips are
    aglow
As a lover's that kindle with kissing, and earth, with
    her raiment and tresses yet wasted and torn,
Takes breath as she smiles in the grasp of thy
    passion to feel through her spirit the sense of
    thee flow.

III

Fain, fain would we see but again for an hour what
    the wind and the sun have dispelled and con-
    sumed,
Those full deep swan-soft feathers of snow with
    whose luminous burden the branches implumed
Hung heavily, curved as a half-bent bow, and fledged
    not as birds are, but petalled as flowers,
Each tree-top and branchlet a pinnacle jewelled and
    carved, or a fountain that shines as it showers,
But fixed as a fountain is fixed not, and wrought not
    to last till by time or by tempest entombed,

As a pinnacle carven and gilded of men : for the date
    of its doom is no more than an hour's,
One hour of the sun's when the warm wind wakes
    him to wither the snow-flowers that froze as they
    bloomed.

IV

As the sunshine quenches the snowshine ; as April
    subdues thee, and yields up his kingdom to
    May ;
So time overcomes the regret that is born of delight
    as it passes in passion away,
And leaves but a dream for desire to rejoice in or
    mourn for with tears or thanksgivings ; but
    thou,
Bright god that art gone from us, maddest and
    gladdest of months, to what goal hast thou gone
    from us now ?
For somewhere surely the storm of thy laughter that
    lightens, the beat of thy wings that play,
Must flame as a fire through the world, and the
    heavens that we know not rejoice in thee : surely
    thy brow
Hath lost not its radiance of empire, thy spirit the
    joy that impelled it on quest as for prey.

V

Are thy feet on the ways of the limitless waters, thy
    wings on the winds of the waste north sea ?
Are the fires of the false north dawn over heavens
    where summer is stormful and strong like thee

Now bright in the sight of thine eyes? are the
 bastions of icebergs assailed by the blast of thy
 breath?
Is it March with the wild north world when April is
 waning? the word that the changed year saith,
Is it echoed to northward with rapture of passion
 reiterate from spirits triumphant as we
Whose hearts were uplift at the blast of thy clarions
 as men's rearisen from a sleep that was death
And kindled to life that was one with the world's and
 with thine? hast thou set not the whole world
 free?

VI

For the breath of thy lips is freedom, and freedom's
 the sense of thy spirit, the sound of thy song,
Glad god of the north-east wind, whose heart is as
 high as the hands of thy kingdom are strong,
Thy kingdom whose empire is terror and joy, twin-
 featured and fruitful of births divine,
Days lit with the flame of the lamps of the flowers,
 and nights that are drunken with dew for wine,
And sleep not for joy of the stars that deepen and
 quicken, a denser and fierier throng,
And the world that thy breath bade whiten and
 tremble rejoices at heart as they strengthen and
 shine,
And earth gives thanks for the glory bequeathed
 her, and knows of thy reign that it wrought not
 wrong.

VII

Thy spirit is quenched not, albeit we behold not thy
    face in the crown of the steep sky's arch,
And the bold first buds of the whin wax golden, and
    witness arise of the thorn and the larch :
Wild April, enkindled to laughter and storm by the
    kiss of the wildest of winds that blow,
Calls loud on his brother for witness ; his hands
    that were laden with blossom are sprinkled with
    snow,
And his lips breathe winter, and laugh, and relent ;
    and the live woods feel not the frost's flame
    parch ;
For the flame of the spring that consumes not but
    quickens is felt at the heart of the forest aglow,
And the sparks that enkindled and fed it were strewn
    from the hands of the gods of the winds of
    March.

THE COMMONWEAL

1887

I

EIGHT hundred years and twenty-one
   Have shone and sunken since the land
   Whose name is freedom bore such brand
As marks a captive, and the sun
   Beheld her fettered hand.

II

But ere dark time had shed as rain
   Or sown on sterile earth as seed
   That bears no fruit save tare and weed
An age and half an age again,
   She rose on Runnymede.

III

Out of the shadow, starlike still,
   She rose up radiant in her right,
   And spake, and put to fear and flight
The lawless rule of awless will
   That pleads no right save might.

IV

Nor since hath England ever borne
    The burden laid on subject lands,
    The rule that curbs and binds all hands
Save one, and marks for servile scorn
    The heads it bows and brands.

V

A commonweal arrayed and crowned
    With gold and purple, girt with steel
    At need, that foes must fear or feel,
We find her, as our fathers found,
    Earth's lordliest commonweal.

VI

And now that fifty years are flown
    Since in a maiden's hand the sign
    Of empire that no seas confine
First as a star to seaward shone,
    We see their record shine.

VII

A troubled record, foul and fair,
    A simple record and serene,
    Inscribes for praise a blameless queen,
For praise and blame an age of care
    And change and ends unseen.

VIII

Hope, wide of eye and wild of wing,
　　Rose with the sundawn of a reign
　　Whose grace should make the rough ways plain,
And fill the worn old world with spring,
　　And heal its heart of pain.

IX

Peace was to be on earth ; men's hope
　　Was holier than their fathers had,
　　Their wisdom not more wise than glad :
They saw the gates of promise ope,
　　And heard what love's lips bade.

X

Love armed with knowledge, winged and wise,
　　Should hush the wind of war, and see,
　　They said, the sun of days to be
Bring round beneath serener skies
　　A stormless jubilee.

XI

Time, in the darkness unbeholden
　　That hides him from the sight of fear
　　And lets but dreaming hope draw near,
Smiled and was sad to hear such golden
　　Strains hail the all-golden year.

XII

Strange clouds have risen between, and wild
   Red stars of storm that lit the abyss
   Wherein fierce fraud and violence kiss
And mock such promise as beguiled
   The fiftieth year from this.

XIII

War upon war, change after change,
   Hath shaken thrones and towers to dust,
   And hopes austere and faiths august
Have watched in patience stern and strange
   Men's works unjust and just.

XIV

As from some Alpine watch-tower's portal
   Night, living yet, looks forth for dawn,
   So from time's mistier mountain lawn
The spirit of man, in trust immortal,
   Yearns toward a hope withdrawn.

XV

The morning comes not, yet the night
   Wanes, and men's eyes win strength to see
   Where twilight is, where light shall be
When conquered wrong and conquering right
   Acclaim a world set free.

XVI

Calm as our mother-land, the mother
   Of faith and freedom, pure and wise,
   Keeps watch beneath unchangeful skies,
When hath she watched the woes of other
   Strange lands with alien eyes?

XVII

Calm as she stands alone, what nation
   Hath lacked an alms from English hands?
   What exiles from what stricken lands
Have lacked the shelter of the station
   Where higher than all she stands?

XVIII

Though time discrown and change dismantle
   The pride of thrones and towers that frown,
   How should they bring her glories down—
The sea cast round her like a mantle,
   The sea-cloud like a crown?

XIX

The sea, divine as heaven and deathless,
   Is hers, and none but only she
   Hath learnt the sea's word, none but we
Her children hear in heart the breathless
   Bright watchword of the sea.

XX

Heard not of others, or misheard
　Of many a land for many a year,
　The watchword Freedom fails not here
Of hearts that witness if the word
　Find faith in England's ear.

XXI

She, first to love the light, and daughter
　Incarnate of the northern dawn,
　She, round whose feet the wild waves fawn
When all their wrath of warring water
　Sounds like a babe's breath drawn,

XXII

How should not she best know, love best,
　And best of all souls understand
　The very soul of freedom, scanned
Far off, sought out in darkling quest
　By men at heart unmanned?

XXIII

They climb and fall, ensnared, enshrouded,
　By mists of words and toils they set
　To take themselves, till fierce regret
Grows mad with shame, and all their clouded
　Red skies hang sunless yet.

XXIV

But us the sun, not wholly risen
   Nor equal now for all, illumes
   With more of light than cloud that looms;
Of light that leads forth souls from prison
   And breaks the seals of tombs.

XXV

Did not her breasts who reared us rear
   Him who took heaven in hand, and weighed
   Bright world with world in balance laid?
What Newton's might could make not clear
   Hath Darwin's might not made?

XXVI

The forces of the dark dissolve,
   The doorways of the dark are broken:
   The word that casts out night is spoken,
And whence the springs of things evolve
   Light born of night bears token.

XXVII

She, loving light for light's sake only,
   And truth for only truth's, and song
   For song's sake and the sea's, how long
Hath she not borne the world her lonely
   Witness of right and wrong?

XXVIII

From light to light her eyes imperial
  Turn, and require the further light,
  More perfect than the sun's in sight,
Till star and sun seem all funereal
  Lamps of the vaulted night.

XXIX

She gazes till the strenuous soul
  Within the rapture of her eyes
  Creates or bids awake, arise,
The light she looks for, pure and whole
  And worshipped of the wise.

XXX

Such sons are hers, such radiant hands
  Have borne abroad her lamp of old,
  Such mouths of honey-dropping gold
Have sent across all seas and lands
  Her fame as music rolled.

XXXI

As music made of rolling thunder
  That hurls through heaven its heart sublime,
  Its heart of joy, in charging chime,
So ring the songs that round and under
  Her temple surge and climb.

XXXII

A temple not by men's hands builded,
　But moulded of the spirit, and wrought
　Of passion and imperious thought ;
With light beyond all sunlight gilded,
　Whereby the sun seems nought.

XXXIII

Thy shrine, our mother, seen for fairer
　Than even thy natural face, made fair
　With kisses of thine April air
Even now, when spring thy banner-bearer
　Took up thy sign to bear ;

XXXIV

Thine annual sign from heaven's own arch
　Given of the sun's hand into thine,
　To rear and cheer each wildwood shrine
But now laid waste by wild-winged March,
　March, mad with wind like wine.

XXXV

From all thy brightening downs whereon
　The windy seaward whin-flower shows
　Blossom whose pride strikes pale the rose
Forth is the golden watchword gone
　Whereat the world's face glows.

XXXVI

Thy quickening woods rejoice and ring
　Till earth seems glorious as the sea :
　With yearning love too glad for glee
The world's heart quivers toward the spring
　As all our hearts toward thee.

XXXVII

Thee, mother, thee, our queen, who givest
　Assurance to the heavens most high
　And earth whereon her bondsmen sigh
That by the sea's grace while thou livest
　Hope shall not wholly die.

XXXVIII

That while thy free folk hold the van
　Of all men, and the sea-spray shed
　As dew more heavenly on thy head
Keeps bright thy face in sight of man,
　Man's pride shall drop not dead.

XXXIX

A pride more pure than humblest prayer,
　More wise than wisdom born of doubt,
　Girds for thy sake men's hearts about
With trust and triumph that despair
　And fear may cast not out.

XL

Despair may wring men's hearts, and fear
  Bow down their heads to kiss the dust,
  Where patriot memories rot and rust,
And change makes faint a nation's cheer,
  And faith yields up her trust.

XLI

Not here this year have true men known,
  Not here this year may true men know,
  That brand of shame-compelling woe
Which bids but brave men shrink or groan
  And lays but honour low.

XLII

The strong spring wind blows notes of praise,
  And hallowing pride of heart, and cheer
  Unchanging, toward all true men here
Who hold the trust of ancient days
  High as of old this year.

XLIII

The days that made thee great are dead ;
  The days that now must keep thee great
  Lie not in keeping of thy fate ;
In thine they lie, whose heart and head
  Sustain thy charge of state.

XLIV

No state so proud, no pride so just,
   The sun, through clouds at sunrise curled
   Or clouds across the sunset whirled,
Hath sight of, nor has man such trust
   As thine in all the world.

XLV

Each hour that sees the sunset's crest
   Make bright thy shores ere day decline
   Sees dawn the sun on shores of thine,
Sees west as east and east as west
   On thee their sovereign shine.

XLVI

The sea's own heart must needs wax proud
   To have borne the world a child like thee.
   What birth of earth might ever be
Thy sister?   Time, a wandering cloud,
   Is sunshine on thy sea.

XLVII

Change mars not her; and thee, our mother,
   What change that irks or moves thee mars?
   What shock that shakes? what chance that
      jars?
Time gave thee, as he gave none other,
   A station like a star's.

XLVIII

The storm that shrieks, the wind that wages
  War with the wings of hopes that climb
  Too high toward heaven in doubt sublime,
Assail not thee, approved of ages
  The towering crown of time.

XLIX

Toward thee this year thy children turning
  With souls uplift of changeless cheer
  Salute with love that casts out fear,
With hearts for beacons round thee burning,
  The token of this year.

L

With just and sacred jubilation
  Let earth sound answer to the sea
  For witness, blown on winds as free,
How England, how her crowning nation,
  Acclaims this jubilee.

THE ARMADA

1588 : 1888

I

ENGLAND, mother born of seamen, daughter fostered
    of the sea,
Mother more beloved than all who bear not all their
    children free,
   Reared and nursed and crowned and cherished by
    the sea-wind and the sun,
   Sweetest land and strongest, face most fair and
    mightiest heart in one,
Stands not higher than when the centuries known of
    earth were less by three,
   When the strength that struck the whole world
    pale fell back from hers undone.

II

At her feet were the heads of her foes bowed down,
    and the strengths of the storm of them stayed,
And the hearts that were touched not with mercy with
    terror were touched and amazed and affrayed :

Yea, hearts that had never been molten with pity
    were molten with fear as with flame,
And the priests of the Godhead whose temple is hell,
    and his heart is of iron and fire,
And the swordsmen that served and the seamen that
    sped them, whom peril could tame not or tire,
    Were as foam on the winds of the waters of
    England which tempest can tire not or tame.

III

They were girded about with thunder, and lightning
    came forth of the rage of their strength,
And the measure that measures the wings of the storm
    was the breadth of their force and the length :
And the name of their might was Invincible, covered
    and clothed with the terror of God ;
With his wrath were they winged, with his love were
    they fired, with the speed of his winds were they
    shod ;
With his soul were they filled, in his trust were they
    comforted : grace was upon them as night,
And faith as the blackness of darkness : the fume of
    their balefires was fair in his sight,
The reek of them sweet as a savour of myrrh in his
    nostrils : the world that he made,
Theirs was it by gift of his servants : the wind, if
    they spake in his name, was afraid,
And the sun was a shadow before it, the stars were
    astonished with fear of it : fire
Went up to them, fed with men living, and lit of
    men's hands for a shrine or a pyre ;
And the east and the west wind scattered their ashes
    abroad, that his name should be blest
Of the tribes of the chosen whose blessings are curses
    from uttermost east unto west.

II

I

Hell for Spain, and heaven for England,—God to
    God, and man to man,—
Met confronted, light with darkness, life with death :
    since time began,
  Never earth nor sea beheld so great a stake before
    them set,
  Save when Athens hurled back Asia from the lists
    wherein they met ;
Never since the sands of ages through the glass of
    history ran
  Saw the sun in heaven a lordlier day than this
    that lights us yet.

II

For the light that abides upon England, the glory
    that rests on her godlike name,
The pride that is love and the love that is faith, a
    perfume dissolved in flame,
  Took fire from the dawn of the fierce July when
    fleets were scattered as foam
And squadrons as flakes of spray ; when galleon and
    galliass that shadowed the sea
Were swept from her waves like shadows that pass
    with the clouds they fell from, and she
  Laughed loud to the wind as it gave to her keeping
    the glories of Spain and Rome.

III

Three hundred summers have fallen as leaves by the
    storms in their season thinned,
Since northward the war-ships of Spain came sheer
    up the way of the south-west wind :
Where the citadel cliffs of England are flanked with
    bastions of serpentine,
Far off to the windward loomed their hulls, an
    hundred and twenty-nine,
All filled full of the war, full-fraught with battle and
    charged with bale ;
Then store-ships weighted with cannon ; and all were
    an hundred and fifty sail.
The measureless menace of darkness anhungered
    with hope to prevail upon light,
The shadow of death made substance, the present
    and visible spirit of night,
Came, shaped as a waxing or waning moon that rose
    with the fall of day,
To the channel where couches the Lion in guard of
    the gate of the lustrous bay.
Fair England, sweet as the sea that shields her, and
    pure as the sea from stain,
Smiled, hearing hardly for scorn that stirred her the
    menace of saintly Spain.

III

I

" They that ride over ocean wide with hempen bridle
    and horse of tree,"
How shall they in the darkening day of wrath and
    anguish and fear go free ?
How shall these that have curbed the seas not feel
    his bridle who made the sea ?

God shall bow them and break them now : for what
    is man in the Lord God's sight ?
Fear shall shake them, and shame shall break, and
    all the noon of their pride be night :
These that sinned shall the ravening wind of doom
    bring under, and judgment smite.

England broke from her neck the yoke, and rent the
    fetter, and mocked the rod :
Shrines of old that she decked with gold she turned
    to dust, to the dust she trod :
What is she, that the wind and sea should fight
    beside her, and war with God ?

Lo, the cloud of his ships that crowd her channel's
    inlet with storm sublime,
Darker far than the tempests are that sweep the skies
    of her northmost clime ;
Huge and dense as the walls that fence the secret
    darkness of unknown time.

Mast on mast as a tower goes past, and sail by sail
    as a cloud's wing spread ;
Fleet by fleet, as the throngs whose feet keep time
    with death in his dance of dread ;
Galleons dark as the helmsman's bark of old that
    ferried to hell the dead.

Squadrons proud as their lords, and loud with tramp
    of soldiers and chant of priests ;
Slaves there told by the thousandfold, made fast in
    bondage as herded beasts ;
Lords and slaves that the sweet free waves shall feed
    on, satiate with funeral feasts.

Nay, not so shall it be, they know ; their priests have
    said it ; can priesthood lie ?
God shall keep them, their God shall sleep not : peril
    and evil shall pass them by :
Nay, for these are his children ; seas and winds shall
    bid not his children die.

II

So they boast them, the monstrous host whose
    menace mocks at the dawn : and here
They that wait at the wild sea's gate, and watch the
    darkness of doom draw near,
How shall they in their evil day sustain the strength
    of their hearts for fear ?

Full July in the fervent sky sets forth her twentieth
    of changing morns :
Winds fall mild that of late waxed wild : no presage
    whispers or wails or warns :
Far to west on the bland sea's breast a sailing crescent
    uprears her horns.

Seven wide miles the serene sea smiles between them
    stretching from rim to rim :
Soft they shine, but a darker sign should bid not
    hope or belief wax dim :
God's are these men, and not the sea's : their trust
    is set not on her but him.

God's ? but who is the God whereto the prayers and
    incense of these men rise ?
What is he, that the wind and sea should fear him,
    quelled by his sunbright eyes ?
What, that men should return again, and hail him
    Lord of the servile skies ?

Hell's own flame at his heavenly name leaps higher
    and laughs, and its gulfs rejoice :
Plague and death from his baneful breath take life
    and lighten, and praise his choice :
Chosen are they to devour for prey the tribes that
    hear not and fear his voice.

Ay, but we that the wind and sea gird round with
    shelter of storms and waves
Know not him that ye worship, grim as dreams that
    quicken from dead men's graves :
God is one with the sea, the sun, the land that nursed
    us, the love that saves.

Love whose heart is in ours, and part of all things
    noble and all things fair ;
Sweet and free as the circling sea, sublime and kind
    as the fostering air ;
Pure of shame as is England's name, whose crowns
    to come are as crowns that were.

VOL. III.   O

IV

I

But the Lord of darkness, the God whose love is a
　　　flaming fire,
The master whose mercy fulfils wide hell till its
　　　torturers tire,
He shall surely have heed of his servants who serve
　　　him for love, not hire.

They shall fetter the wing of the wind whose pinions
　　　are plumed with foam :
For now shall thy horn be exalted, and now shall thy
　　　bolt strike home ;
Yea, now shall thy kingdom come, Lord God of the
　　　priests of Rome.

They shall cast thy curb on the waters, and bridle
　　　the waves of the sea :
They shall say to her, Peace, be still : and stillness
　　　and peace shall be :
And the winds and the storms shall hear them, and
　　　tremble, and worship thee.

Thy breath shall darken the morning, and wither the
　　　mounting sun ;
And the daysprings, frozen and fettered, shall know
　　　thee, and cease to run ;
The heart of the world shall feel thee, and die, and
　　　thy will be done.

The spirit of man that would sound thee, and search
  out causes of things,
Shall shrink and subside and praise thee : and wisdom,
  with plume-plucked wings,
Shall cower at thy feet and confess thee, that none
  may fathom thy springs.

The fountains of song that await but the wind of an
  April to be
To burst the bonds of the winter, and speak with the
  sound of a sea,
The blast of thy mouth shall quench them : and song
  shall be only of thee.

The days that are dead shall quicken, the seasons
  that were shall return ;
And the streets and the pastures of England, the
  woods that burgeon and yearn,
Shall be whitened with ashes of women and children
  and men that burn.

For the mother shall burn with the babe sprung forth
  of her womb in fire,
And bride with bridegroom, and brother with sister,
  and son with sire ;
And the noise of the flames shall be sweet in thine
  ears as the sound of a lyre.

Yea, so shall thy kingdom be stablished, and so shall
  the signs of it be :
And the world shall know, and the wind shall speak,
  and the sun shall see,
That these are the works of thy servants, whose
  works bear witness to thee.

II

But the dusk of the day falls fruitless, whose light
  should have lit them on :
Sails flash through the gloom to shoreward, eclipsed
  as the sun that shone :
And the west wind wakes with dawn, and the hope
  that was here is gone.

Around they wheel and around, two knots to the
  Spaniard's one,
The wind-swift warriors of England, who shoot as
  with shafts of the sun,
With fourfold shots for the Spaniard's, that spare
  not till day be done.

And the wind with the sundown sharpens, and hurtles
  the ships to the lee,
And Spaniard on Spaniard smites, and shatters, and
  yields ; and we,
Ere battle begin, stand lords of the battle, acclaimed
  of the sea.

And the day sweeps round to the nightward ; and
  heavy and hard the waves
Roll in on the herd of the hurtling galleons ; and
  masters and slaves
Reel blind in the grasp of the dark strong wind that
  shall dig their graves.

For the sepulchres hollowed and shaped of the wind
  in the swerve of the seas,
The graves that gape for their pasture, and laugh,
  thrilled through by the breeze,
The sweet soft merciless waters, await and are fain
  of these.

As the hiss of a Python heaving in menace of doom
    to be
They hear through the clear night round them,
    whose hours are as clouds that flee,
The whisper of tempest sleeping, the heave and the
    hiss of the sea.

But faith is theirs, and with faith are they girded
    and helmed and shod :
Invincible are they, almighty, elect for a sword and
    a rod ;
Invincible even as their God is omnipotent, infinite,
    God.

In him is their strength, who have sworn that his
    glory shall wax not dim :
In his name are their war-ships hallowed as mightiest
    of all that swim :
The men that shall cope with these, and conquer,
    shall cast out him.

In him is the trust of their hearts ; the desire of their
    eyes is he ;
The light of their ways, made lightning for men
    that would fain be free :
Earth's hosts are with them, and with them is heaven :
    but with us is the sea.

V

I

And a day and a night pass over ;
    And the heart of their chief swells high ;
For England, the warrior, the rover,
    Whose banners on all winds fly,
Soul-stricken, he saith, by the shadow of death, holds
    off him, and draws not nigh.

And the wind and the dawn together
    Make in from the gleaming east :
And fain of the wild glad weather
    As famine is fain of feast,
And fain of the fight, forth sweeps in its might the
    host of the Lord's high priest.

And lightly before the breeze
    The ships of his foes take wing :
Are they scattered, the lords of the seas ?
    Are they broken, the foes of the king ?
And ever now higher as a mounting fire the hopes of
    the Spaniard spring.

And a windless night comes down :
    And a breezeless morning, bright
With promise of praise to crown
    The close of the crowning fight,
Leaps up as the foe's heart leaps, and glows with
    lustrous rapture of light.

And stinted of gear for battle
   The ships of the sea's folk lie,
Unwarlike, herded as cattle,
   Six miles from the foeman's eye
That fastens as flame on the sight of them tame and
   offenceless, and ranged as to die.

Surely the souls in them quail,
   They are stricken and withered at heart,
When in on them, sail by sail,
   Fierce marvels of monstrous art,
Tower darkening on tower till the sea-winds cower
   crowds down as to hurl them apart.

And the windless weather is kindly,
   And comforts the host in these ;
And their hearts are uplift in them blindly,
   And blindly they boast at ease
That the next day's fight shall exalt them, and smite
   with destruction the lords of the seas.

II

And lightly the proud hearts prattle,
   And lightly the dawn draws nigh,
The dawn of the doom of the battle
   When these shall falter and fly ;
No day more great in the roll of fate filled ever with
   fire the sky.

To fightward they go as to feastward,
   And the tempest of ships that drive
Sets eastward ever and eastward,
   Till closer they strain and strive ;
And the shots that rain on the hulls of Spain are as
   thunders afire and alive.

And about them the blithe sea smiles
　　And flashes to windward and lee
Round capes and headlands and isles
　　That heed not if war there be ;
Round Sark, round Wight, green jewels of light in
　　the ring of the golden sea.

But the men that within them abide
　　Are stout of spirit and stark
As rocks that repel the tide,
　　As day that repels the dark ;
And the light bequeathed from their swords unsheathed
　　shines lineal on Wight and on Sark.

And eastward the storm sets ever,
　　The storm of the sails that strain
And follow and close and sever
　　And lose and return and gain ;
And English thunder divides in sunder the holds of
　　the ships of Spain.

Southward to Calais, appalled
　　And astonished, the vast fleet veers ;
And the skies are shrouded and palled,
　　But the moonless midnight hears
And sees how swift on them drive and drift strange
　　flames that the darkness fears.

They fly through the night from shoreward,
　　Heart-stricken till morning break,
And ever to scourge them forward
　　Drives down on them England's Drake,
And hurls them in as they hurtle and spin and stagger,
　　with storm to wake.

They sink in the whelm of the waters, as pebbles by
children from shoreward hurled,

In the North Sea's waters that end not, nor
know they a bourn but the bourn of the
world.

Past many a secure unavailable harbour, and many
a loud stream's mouth,

Past Humber and Tees and Tyne and Tweed, they
fly, scourged on from the south,

And torn by the scourge of the storm-wind that
smites as a harper smites on a lyre,

And consumed of the storm as the sacrifice loved of
their God is consumed with fire,

And devoured of the darkness as men that are slain
in the fires of his love are devoured,

And deflowered of their lives by the storms, as by
priests is the spirit of life deflowered.

For the wind, of its godlike mercy, relents not, and
hounds them ahead to the north,

With English hunters at heel, till now is the herd of
them past the Forth,

All huddled and hurtled seaward ; and now need none
wage war upon these,

Nor huntsmen follow the quarry whose fall is the
pastime sought of the seas.

Day upon day upon day confounds them, with
measureless mists that swell,

With drift of rains everlasting and dense as the fumes
of ascending hell.

The visions of priest and of prophet beholding his
enemies bruised of his rod

Beheld but the likeness of this that is fallen on the
faithful, the friends of God.

Northward, and northward, and northward they
    stagger and shudder and swerve and flit,

Dismantled of masts and of yards, with sails by the
    fangs of the storm-wind split.

But north of the headland whose name is Wrath, by
    the wrath or the ruth of the sea,

They are swept or sustained to the westward, and
    drive through the rollers aloof to the lee.

Some strive yet northward for Iceland, and perish :
    but some through the storm-hewn straits

That sunder the Shetlands and Orkneys are borne of
    the breath which is God's or fate's :

And some, by the dawn of September, at last give
    thanks as for stars that smile,

For the winds have swept them to shelter and sight
    of the cliffs of a Catholic isle.

Though many the fierce rocks feed on, and many the
    merciless heretic slays,

Yet some that have laboured to land with their
    treasure are trustful, and give God praise.

And the kernes of murderous Ireland, athirst with a
    greed everlasting of blood,

Unslakable ever with slaughter and spoil, rage down
    as a ravening flood,

To slay and to flay of their shining apparel their
    brethren whom shipwreck spares ;

Such faith and such mercy, such love and such
    manhood, such hands and such hearts are theirs.

Short shrift to her foes gives England, but shorter
    doth Ireland to friends ; and worse

Fare they that came with a blessing on treason than
    they that come with a curse.

Hacked, harried, and mangled of axes and skenes,
    three thousand naked and dead

Bear witness of Catholic Ireland, what sons of what
    sires at her breasts are bred.

Winds are pitiful, waves are merciful, tempest and
    storm are kind :

The waters that smite may spare, and the thunder is
    deaf, and the lightning is blind :

Of these perchance at his need may a man, though
    they know it not, yet find grace ;

But grace, if another be hardened against him, he
    gets not at this man's face.

For his ear that hears and his eye that sees the wreck
    and the wail of men,

And his heart that relents not within him, but
    hungers, are like as the wolf's in his den.

Worthy are these to worship their master, the
    murderous Lord of lies,

Who hath given to the pontiff his servant the keys of
    the pit and the keys of the skies.

Wild famine and red-shod rapine are cruel, and bitter
    with blood are their feasts ;

But fiercer than famine and redder than rapine the
    hands and the hearts of priests.

God, God bade these to the battle ; and here, on a
    land by his servants trod,

They perish, a lordly blood-offering, subdued by the
    hands of the servants of God.

These also were fed of his priests with faith, with the
    milk of his word and the wine ;

These too are fulfilled with the spirit of darkness that
    guided their quest divine.

And here, cast up from the ravening sea on the mild
    land's merciful breast,
This comfort they find of their fellows in worship ;
    this guerdon is theirs of their quest.
Death was captain, and doom was pilot, and darkness
    the chart of their way ;
Night and hell had in charge and in keeping the host
    of the foes of day.
Invincible, vanquished, impregnable, shattered, a sign
    to her foes of fear,
A sign to the world and the stars of laughter, the
    fleet of the Lord lies here.
Nay, for none may declare the place of the ruin
    wherein she lies ;
Nay, for none hath beholden the grave whence never
    a ghost shall rise.
The fleet of the foemen of England hath found not
    one but a thousand graves ;
And he that shall number and name them shall
    number by name and by tale the waves.

VII

I

Sixtus, Pope of the Church whose hope takes flight
    for heaven to dethrone the sun,
Philip, king that wouldst turn our spring to winter,
    blasted, appalled, undone,
Prince and priest, let a mourner's feast give thanks
    to God for your conquest won.

England's heel is upon you : kneel, O priest, O prince,
    in the dust, and cry,
" Lord, why thus ? art thou wroth with us whose
    faith was great in thee, God most high ?
Whence is this, that the serpent's hiss derides us ?
    Lord, can thy pledged word lie ?

" God of hell, are its flames that swell quenched now
    for ever, extinct and dead ?
Who shall fear thee ? or who shall hear the word thy
    servants who feared thee said ?
Lord, art thou as the dead gods now, whose arm is
    shortened, whose rede is read ?

" Yet we thought it was not for nought thy word was
    given us, to guard and guide :
Yet we deemed that they had not dreamed who put
    their trust in thee.   Hast thou lied ?
God our Lord, was the sacred sword we drew not
    drawn on thy Church's side ?

" England hates thee as hell's own gates ; and England
    triumphs, and Rome bows down :
England mocks at thee ; England's rocks cast off thy
    servants to drive and drown :
England loathes thee ; and fame betroths and plights
    with England her faith for crown.

" Spain clings fast to thee ; Spain, aghast with
    anguish, cries to thee ; where art thou ?
Spain puts trust in thee ; lo, the dust that soils and
    darkens her prostrate brow !
Spain is true to thy service ; who shall raise up Spain
    for thy service now ?

" Who shall praise thee, if none may raise thy servants
    up, nor affright thy foes ?
Winter wanes, and the woods and plains forget the
    likeness of storms and snows :
So shall fear of thee fade even here : and what shall
    follow thee no man knows."

Lords of night, who would breathe your blight on
    April's morning and August's noon,
God your Lord, the condemned, the abhorred, sinks
    hellward, smitten with deathlike swoon :
Death's own dart in his hateful heart now thrills, and
    night shall receive him soon.

God the Devil, thy reign of revel is here for ever
    eclipsed and fled :
God the Liar, everlasting fire lays hold at last on thee,
    hand and head :
God the Accurst, the consuming thirst that burns
    thee never shall here be fed.

II

England, queen of the waves whose green inviolate
    girdle enrings thee round,
Mother fair as the morning, where is now the place
    of thy foemen found ?
Still the sea that salutes us free proclaims them
    stricken, acclaims thee crowned.

Times may change, and the skies grow strange with
    signs of treason and fraud and fear :
Foes in union of strange communion may rise against
    thee from far and near :
Sloth and greed on thy strength may feed as cankers
    waxing from year to year.

Yet, though treason and fierce unreason should league
  and lie and defame and smite,
We that know thee, how far below thee the hatred
  burns of the sons of night,
We that love thee, behold above thee the witness
  written of life in light.

Life that shines from thee shows forth signs that
  none may read not but eyeless foes :
Hate, born blind, in his abject mind grows hopeful
  now but as madness grows :
Love, born wise, with exultant eyes adores thy glory,
  beholds and glows.

Truth is in thee, and none may win thee to lie, for-
  saking the face of truth :
Freedom lives by the grace she gives thee, born again
  from thy deathless youth :
Faith should fail, and the world turn pale, wert thou
  the prey of the serpent's tooth.

Greed and fraud, unabashed, unawed, may strive to
  sting thee at heel in vain :
Craft and fear and mistrust may leer and mourn and
  murmur and plead and plain :
Thou art thou : and thy sunbright brow is hers that
  blasted the strength of Spain.

Mother, mother beloved, none other could claim in
  place of thee England's place :
Earth bears none that beholds the sun so pure of
  record, so clothed with grace :
Dear our mother, nor son nor brother is thine, as
  strong or as fair of face.

How shalt thou be abased ? or how shall fear take
hold of thy heart ? of thine,
England, maiden immortal, laden with charge of life
and with hopes divine?
Earth shall wither, when eyes turned hither behold
not light in her darkness shine.

England, none that is born thy son, and lives, by
grace of thy glory, free,
Lives and yearns not at heart and burns with hope
to serve as he worships thee ;
None may sing thee : the sea-wind's wing beats down
our songs as it hails the sea.

TO A SEAMEW

When I had wings, my brother,
  Such wings were mine as thine:
Such life my heart remembers
In all as wild Septembers
As this when life seems other,
  Though sweet, than once was mine;
When I had wings, my brother,
  Such wings were mine as thine.

Such life as thrills and quickens
  The silence of thy flight,
Or fills thy note's elation
With lordlier exultation
Than man's, whose faint heart sickens
  With hopes and fears that blight
Such life as thrills and quickens
  The silence of thy flight.

Thy cry from windward clanging
  Makes all the cliffs rejoice;
Though storm clothe seas with sorrow,
Thy call salutes the morrow;
While shades of pain seem hanging
  Round earth's most rapturous voice,
Thy cry from windward clanging
  Makes all the cliffs rejoice.

We, sons and sires of seamen,
  Whose home is all the sea,
What place man may, we claim it ;
But thine—whose thought may name it ?
Free birds live higher than freemen,
  And gladlier ye than we—
We, sons and sires of seamen,
  Whose home is all the sea.

For you the storm sounds only
  More notes of more delight
Than earth's in sunniest weather :
When heaven and sea together
Join strengths against the lonely
  Lost bark borne down by night,
For you the storm sounds only
  More notes of more delight.

With wider wing, and louder
  Long clarion-call of joy,
Thy tribe salutes the terror
Of darkness, wild as error,
But sure as truth, and prouder
  Than waves with man for toy ;
With wider wing, and louder
  Long clarion-call of joy.

The wave's wing spreads and flutters,
  The wave's heart swells and breaks ;
One moment's passion thrills it,
One pulse of power fulfils it
And ends the pride it utters
  When, loud with life that quakes,
The wave's wing spreads and flutters,
  The wave's heart swells and breaks.

But thine and thou, my brother,
  Keep heart and wing more high
Than aught may scare or sunder ;
The waves whose throats are thunder
Fall hurtling each on other,
  And triumph as they die ;
But thine and thou, my brother,
  Keep heart and wing more high.

More high than wrath or anguish,
  More strong than pride or fear,
The sense or soul half hidden
In thee, for us forbidden,
Bids thee nor change nor languish,
  But live thy life as here,
More high than wrath or anguish,
  More strong than pride or fear.

We are fallen, even we, whose passion
  On earth is nearest thine ;
Who sing, and cease from flying ;
Who live, and dream of dying :
Grey time, in time's grey fashion,
  Bids wingless creatures pine :
We are fallen, even we, whose passion
  On earth is nearest thine.

The lark knows no such rapture,
  Such joy no nightingale,
As sways the songless measure
Wherein thy wings take pleasure :
Thy love may no man capture,
  Thy pride may no man quail ;
The lark knows no such rapture,
  Such joy no nightingale.

And we, whom dreams embolden,
  We can but creep and sing
And watch through heaven's waste hollow
The flight no sight may follow
To the utter bourne beholden
  Of none that lack thy wing :
And we, whom dreams embolden,
  We can but creep and sing.

Our dreams have wings that falter,
  Our hearts bear hopes that die ;
For thee no dream could better
A life no fears may fetter,
A pride no care can alter,
  That wots not whence or why
Our dreams have wings that falter,
  Our hearts bear hopes that die.

With joy more fierce and sweeter
  Than joys we deem divine
Their lives, by time untarnished,
Are girt about and garnished,
Who match the wave's full metre
  And drink the wind's wild wine
With joy more fierce and sweeter
  Than joys we deem divine.

Ah, well were I for ever,
  Wouldst thou change lives with me,
And take my song's wild honey,
And give me back thy sunny
Wide eyes that weary never,
  And wings that search the sea ;
Ah, well were I for ever,
  Wouldst thou change lives with me.

Beachy Head: September 1886.

PAN AND THALASSIUS

A LYRICAL IDYL

THALASSIUS

PAN !

PAN

O sea-stray, seed of Apollo,
  What word wouldst thou have with me?
My ways thou wast fain to follow
  Or ever the years hailed thee
    Man.

Now
If August brood on the valleys,
  If satyrs laugh on the lawns,
What part in the wildwood alleys
  Hast thou with the fleet-foot fauns—
    Thou?

See !
Thy feet are a man's—not cloven
  Like these, not light as a boy's :
The tresses and tendrils inwoven
  That lure us, the lure of them cloys
    Thee.

Us
The joy of the wild woods never
  Leaves free of the thirst it slakes :
The wild love throbs in us ever
  That burns in the dense hot brakes
    Thus.

Life,
Eternal, passionate, awless,
  Insatiable, mutable, dear,
Makes all men's law for us lawless :
  We strive not : how should we fear
    Strife ?

We,
The birds and the bright winds know not
  Such joys as are ours in the mild
Warm woodland ; joys such as grow not
  In waste green fields of the wild
    Sea.

No ;
Long since, in the world's wind veering,
  Thy heart was estranged from me :
Sweet Echo shall yield thee not hearing :
  What have we to do with thee ?
    Go.

THALASSIUS

Ay !
Such wrath on thy nostril quivers
  As once in Sicilian heat
Bade herdsmen quail, and the rivers
  Shrank, leaving a path for thy feet
    Dry ?

Nay,
Low down in the hot soft hollow
  Too snakelike hisses thy spleen :
" O sea-stray, seed of Apollo ! "
  What ill hast thou heard or seen ?
    Say.

    Man
Knows well, if he hears beside him
  The snarl of thy wrath at noon,
What evil may soon betide him,
  Or late, if thou smite not soon,
    Pan.

    Me
The sound of thy flute, that flatters
  The woods as they smile and sigh,
Charmed fast as it charms thy satyrs,
  Can charm no faster than I
    Thee.

    Fast
Thy music may charm the splendid
  Wide woodland silence to sleep
With sounds and dreams of thee blended
  And whispers of waters that creep
    Past.

    Here
The spell of thee breathes and passes
  And bids the heart in me pause,
Hushed soft as the leaves and the grasses
  Are hushed if the storm's foot draws
    Near.

Yet
The panic that strikes down strangers
    Transgressing thy ways unaware
Affrights not me nor endangers
    Through dread of thy secret snare
        Set.

PAN

Whence
May man find heart to deride me?
    Who made his face as a star
To shine as a God's beside me?
    Nay, get thee away from us, far
        Hence.

THALASSIUS

Then
Shall no man's heart, as he raises
    A hymn to thy secret head,
Wax great with the godhead he praises:
    Thou, God, shalt be like unto dead
        Men.

PAN

Grace
I take not of men's thanksgiving,
    I crave not of lips that live;
They die, and behold, I am living,
    While they and their dead Gods give
        Place.

THALASSIUS

Yea :
Too lightly the words were spoken
That mourned or mocked at thee dead :
But whose was the word, the token,
The song that answered and said
Nay ?

PAN

Whose
But mine, in the midnight hidden,
Clothed round with the strength of night
And mysteries of things forbidden
For all but the one most bright
Muse ?

THALASSIUS

Hers
Or thine, O Pan, was the token
That gave back empire to thee
When power in thy hands lay broken
As reeds that quake if a bee
Stirs ?

PAN

Whom
Have I in my wide woods need of ?
Urania's limitless eyes
Behold not mine end, though they read of
A word that shall speak to the skies
Doom.

THALASSIUS

She
Gave back to thee kingdom and glory,
  And grace that was thine of yore,
And life to thy leaves, late hoary
  As weeds cast up from the hoar
          Sea.

Song
Can bid faith shine as the morning
  Though light in the world be none :
Death shrinks if her tongue sound warning,
  Night quails, and beholds the sun
          Strong.

PAN

Night
Bare rule over men for ages
  Whose worship wist not of me
And gat but sorrows for wages,
  And hardly for tears could see
          Light.

Call
No more on the starry presence
  Whose light through the long dark swam :
Hold fast to the green world's pleasance :
  For I that am lord of it am
          All.

THALASSIUS

God,
God Pan, from the glad wood's portal
 The breaths of thy song blow sweet :
But woods may be walked in of mortal
 Man's thought, where never thy feet
  Trod.

  Thine
All secrets of growth and of birth are,
 All glories of flower and of tree,
Wheresoever the wonders of earth are ;
 The words of the spell of the sea
  Mine.

A BALLAD OF BATH

LIKE a queen enchanted who may not laugh or weep,
  Glad at heart and guarded from change and care
  like ours,
Girt about with beauty by days and nights that creep
Soft as breathless ripples that softly shoreward sweep,
  Lies the lovely city whose grace no grief deflowers.
Age and grey forgetfulness, time that shifts and
  veers,
Touch not thee, our fairest, whose charm no rival
  nears,
  Hailed as England's Florence of one whose praise
  gives grace,
Landor, once thy lover, a name that love reveres :
  Dawn and noon and sunset are one before thy face.

Dawn whereof we know not, and noon whose fruit
  we reap,
  Garnered up in record of years that fell like flowers,
Sunset liker sunrise along the shining steep
Whence thy fair face lightens, and where thy soft
  springs leap,
  Crown at once and gird thee with grace of guardian
  powers

Loved of men beloved of us, souls that fame inspheres,
All thine air hath music for him who dreams and
    hears ;
  Voices mixed of multitudes, feet of friends that
    pace,
Witness why for ever, if heaven's face clouds or
    clears,
  Dawn and noon and sunset are one before thy face.

Peace hath here found harbourage mild as very
    sleep :
  Not the hills and waters, the fields and wildwood
    bowers,
Smile or speak more tenderly, clothed with peace
    more deep,
Here than memory whispers of days our memories
    keep
  Fast with love and laughter and dreams of
    withered hours.
Bright were these as blossom of old, and thought
    endears
Still the fair soft phantoms that pass with smiles or
    tears,
  Sweet as roseleaves hoarded and dried wherein we
    trace
Still the soul and spirit of sense that lives and cheers :
  Dawn and noon and sunset are one before thy face.

City lulled asleep by the chime of passing years,
Sweeter smiles thy rest than the radiance round thy
    peers ;
  Only love and lovely remembrance here have place.
Time on thee lies lighter than music on men's ears ;
  Dawn and noon and sunset are one before thy face.

IN A GARDEN

BABY, see the flowers !
——Baby sees
Fairer things than these,
Fairer though they be than dreams of ours.

Baby, hear the birds !
——Baby knows
Better songs than those,
Sweeter though they sound than sweetest words.

Baby, see the moon !
——Baby's eyes
Laugh to watch it rise,
Answering light with love and night with noon.

Baby, hear the sea !
——Baby's face
Takes a graver grace,
Touched with wonder what the sound may be.

Baby, see the star !
——Baby's hand
Opens, warm and bland,
Calm in claim of all things fair that are.

Baby, hear the bells !
—Baby's head
Bows, as ripe for bed,
Now the flowers curl round and close their cells.

Baby, flower of light,
Sleep, and see
Brighter dreams than we,
Till good day shall smile away good night.

A RHYME

BABE, if rhyme be none
　　For that sweet small word
Babe, the sweetest one
　　Ever heard,

Right it is and meet
　　Rhyme should keep not true
Time with such a sweet
　　Thing as you.

Meet it is that rhyme
　　Should not gain such grace :
What is April's prime
　　To your face?

What to yours is May's
　　Rosiest smile? what sound
Like your laughter sways
　　All hearts round?

None can tell in metre
　　Fit for ears on earth
What sweet star grew sweeter
　　At your birth.

Wisdom doubts what may be :
Hope, with smile sublime,
Trusts : but neither, baby,
Knows the rhyme.

Wisdom lies down lonely ;
Hope keeps watch from far ;
None but one seer only
Sees the star.

Love alone, with yearning
Heart for astrolabe,
Takes the star's height, burning
O'er the babe.

BABY-BIRD

BABY-BIRD, baby-bird,
  Ne'er a song on earth
May be heard, may be heard,
  Rich as yours in mirth.

All your flickering fingers,
  All your twinkling toes,
Play like light that lingers
  Till the clear song close.

Baby-bird, baby-bird,
  Your grave majestic eyes
Like a bird's warbled words
  Speak, and sorrow dies.

Sorrow dies for love's sake,
  Love grows one with mirth,
Even for one white dove's sake,
  Born a babe on earth.

Baby-bird, baby-bird,
  Chirping loud and long,
Other birds hush their words,
  Hearkening toward your song.

Sweet as spring though it ring,
  Full of love's own lures,
Weak and wrong sounds their song,
  Singing after yours.

Baby-bird, baby-bird,
  The happy heart that hears
Seems to win back within
  Heaven, and cast out fears.

Earth and sun seem as one
  Sweet light and one sweet word
Known of none here but one,
  Known of one sweet bird.

OLIVE

I

WHO may praise her ?
Eyes where midnight shames the sun,
Hair of night and sunshine spun,
Woven of dawn's or twilight's loom,
Radiant darkness, lustrous gloom,
Godlike childhood's flowerlike bloom,
None may praise aright, nor sing
Half the grace wherewith like spring
    Love arrays her.

II

    Love untold
Sings in silence, speaks in light
Shed from each fair feature, bright
Still from heaven, whence toward us, now
Nine years since, she deigned to bow
Down the brightness of her brow,
Deigned to pass through mortal birth :
Reverence calls her, here on earth,
    Nine years old.

III

Love's deep duty,
Even when love transfigured grows
Worship, all too surely knows
How, though love may cast out fear,
Yet the debt divine and dear
Due to childhood's godhead here
May by love of man be paid
Never ; never song be made
  Worth its beauty.

IV

Nought is all
Sung or said or dreamed or thought
Ever, set beside it ; nought
All the love that man may give—
Love whose prayer should be, " Forgive !"
Heaven, we see, on earth may live ;
Earth can thank not heaven, we know,
Save with songs that ebb and flow,
  Rise and fall.

V

No man living,
No man dead, save haply one
Now gone homeward past the sun,
Ever found such grace as might
Tune his tongue to praise aright
Children, flowers of love and light,
Whom our praise dispraises : we
Sing, in sooth, but not as he
  Sang thanksgiving.

VI

Hope that smiled,
Seeing her new-born beauty, made
Out of heaven's own light and shade,
Smiled not half so sweetly : love,
Seeing the sun, afar above,
Warm the nest that rears the dove,
Sees, more bright than moon or sun,
All the heaven of heavens in one
      Little child.

VII

Who may sing her?
Wings of angels when they stir
Make no music worthy her :
Sweeter sound her shy soft words
Here than songs of God's own birds
Whom the fire of rapture girds
Round with light from love's face lit ;
Hands of angels find no fit
      Gifts to bring her.

VIII

Babes at birth
Wear as raiment round them cast,
Keep as witness toward their past,
Tokens left of heaven ; and each,
Ere its lips learn mortal speech,
Ere sweet heaven pass on pass reach,
Bears in undiverted eyes
Proof of unforgotten skies
      Here on earth.

IX

Quenched as embers
Quenched with flakes of rain or snow
Till the last faint flame burns low,
All those lustrous memories lie
Dead with babyhood gone by :
Yet in her they dare not die :
Others, fair as heaven is, yet,
Now they share not heaven, forget :
    She remembers.

A WORD WITH THE WIND.

Lord of days and nights that hear thy word of wintry
    warning,
  Wind, whose feet are set on ways that none may
    tread,
Change the nest wherein thy wings are fledged for
    flight by morning,
  Change the harbour whence at dawn thy sails are
    spread.
Not the dawn, ere yet the imprisoning night has
    half released her,
  More desires the sun's full face of cheer, than we,
Well as yet we love the strength of the iron-tongued
    north-easter,
  Yearn for wind to meet us as we front the sea.
All thy ways are good, O wind, and all the world
    should fester,
  Were thy fourfold godhead quenched, or stilled thy
    strife :
Yet the waves and we desire too long the deep
    south-wester,
  Whence the waters quicken shoreward, clothed
    with life.

Yet the field not made for ploughing save of keels
    nor harrowing
  Save of storm-winds lies unbrightened by thy
    breath :
Banded broad with ruddy samphire glow the sea-
    banks narrowing
  Westward, while the sea gleams chill and still as
    death.
Sharp and strange from inland sounds thy bitter note
    of battle,
  Blown between grim skies and waters sullen-souled,
Till the baffled seas bear back, rocks roar and shingles
    rattle,
  Vexed and angered and anhungered and acold.
Change thy note, and give the waves their will, and
    all the measure,
  Full and perfect, of the music of their might,
Let it fill the bays with thunderous notes and throbs
    of pleasure,
  Shake the shores with passion, sound at once and
    smite.
Sweet are even the mild low notes of wind and sea,
    but sweeter
  Sounds the song whose choral wrath of raging
    rhyme
Bids the shelving shoals keep tune with storm's im-
    perious metre,
  Bids the rocks and reefs respond in rapturous chime.
Sweet the lisp and lulling whisper and luxurious
    laughter,
  Soft as love or sleep, of waves whereon the sun
Dreams, and dreams not of the darkling hours before
    nor after,
  Winged with cloud whose wrath shall bid love's
    day be done.

Yet shall darkness bring the awakening sea a lordlier
    lover,
    Clothed with strength more amorous and more
      strenuous will,
Whence her heart of hearts shall kindle and her soul
    recover
    Sense of love too keen to lie for love's sake still.
Let thy strong south-western music sound, and bid
    the billows
    Brighten, proud and glad to feel thy scourge and
      kiss
Sting and soothe and sway them, bowed as aspens
    bend or willows,
    Yet resurgent still in breathless rage of bliss.
All to-day the slow sleek ripples hardly bear up shore-
    ward,
    Charged with sighs more light than laughter, faint
      and fair,
Like a woodland lake's weak wavelets lightly linger-
    ing forward,
    Soft and listless as the slumber-stricken air.
Be the sunshine bared or veiled, the sky superb or
    shrouded,
    Still the waters, lax and languid, chafed and foiled,
Keen and thwarted, pale and patient, clothed with
    fire or clouded,
    Vex their heart in vain, or sleep like serpents coiled.
Thee they look for, blind and baffled, wan with wrath
    and weary,
    Blown for ever back by winds that rock the bird :
Winds that seamews breast subdue the sea, and bid
    the dreary
    Waves be weak as hearts made sick with hope
      deferred.

Let thy clarion sound from westward, let the south
    bear token
  How the glories of thy godhead sound and shine :
Bid the land rejoice to see the land-wind's broad
    wings broken,
  Bid the sea take comfort, bid the world be thine.
Half the world abhors thee beating back the sea, and
    blackening
  Heaven with fierce and woful change of fluctuant
    form :
All the world acclaims thee shifting sail again, and
    slackening
  Cloud by cloud the close-reefed cordage of the
    storm.
Sweeter fields and brighter woods and lordlier hills
    than waken
  Here at sunrise never hailed the sun and thee :
Turn thee then, and give them comfort, shed like rain
    and shaken
  Far as foam that laughs and leaps along the sea.

NEAP-TIDE

Far off is the sea, and the land is afar:
    The low banks reach at the sky,
    Seen hence, and are heavenward high ;
Though light for the leap of a boy they are,
    And the far sea late was nigh.

The fair wild fields and the circling downs,
    The bright sweet marshes and meads
    All glorious with flowerlike weeds,
The great grey churches, the sea-washed towns,
    Recede as a dream recedes.

The world draws back, and the world's light wanes,
    As a dream dies down and is dead ;
    And the clouds and the gleams overhead
Change, and change ; and the sea remains,
    A shadow of dreamlike dread.

Wild, and woful, and pale, and grey,
    A shadow of sleepless fear,
    A corpse with the night for bier,
The fairest thing that beholds the day
    Lies haggard and hopeless here.

And the wind's wings, broken and spent, subside ;
    And the dumb waste world is hoar,
    And strange as the sea the shore ;
And shadows of shapeless dreams abide
    Where life may abide no more.

A sail to seaward, a sound from shoreward,
    And the spell were broken that seems
    To reign in a world of dreams
Where vainly the dreamer's feet make forward
    And vainly the low sky gleams.

The sea-forsaken forlorn deep-wrinkled
    Salt slanting stretches of sand
    That slope to the seaward hand,
Were they fain of the ripples that flashed and twinkled
    And laughed as they struck the strand ?

As bells on the reins of the fairies ring
    The ripples that kissed them rang,
    The light from the sundawn sprang,
And the sweetest of songs that the world may sing
    Was theirs when the full sea sang.

Now no light is in heaven ; and now
    Not a note of the sea-wind's tune
    Rings hither : the bleak sky's boon
Grants hardly sight of a grey sun's brow—
    A sun more sad than the moon.

More sad than a moon that clouds beleaguer
    And storm is a scourge to smite,
    The sick sun's shadowlike light
Grows faint as the clouds and the waves wax eager,
    And withers away from sight.

The day's heart cowers, and the night's heart
    quickens :
    Full fain would the day be dead
    And the stark night reign in his stead :
The sea falls dumb as the sea-fog thickens
    And the sunset dies for dread.

Outside of the range of time, whose breath
    Is keen as the manslayer's knife
    And his peace but a truce for strife,
Who knows if haply the shadow of death
    May be not the light of life ?

For the storm and the rain and the darkness borrow
    But an hour from the suns to be,
    But a strange swift passage, that we
May rejoice, who have mourned not to-day, to-
    morrow,
    In the sun and the wind and the sea.

BY THE WAYSIDE

SUMMER'S face was rosiest, skies and woods were
    mellow,
Earth had heaven to friend, and heaven had earth to
    fellow,
  When we met where wooded hills and meadows
    meet.
Autumn's face is pale, and all her late leaves yellow,
  Now that here again we greet.

Wan with years whereof this eightieth nears
    December,
  Fair and bright with love, the kind old face I know
Shines above the sweet small twain whose eyes
    remember
Heaven, and fill with April's light this pale November,
  Though the dark year's glass run low.

Like a rose whose joy of life her silence utters
When the birds are loud, and low the lulled wind
    mutters,
  Grave and silent shines the boy nigh three years
    old.
Wise and sweet his smile, that falters not nor flutters,
  Glows, and turns the gloom to gold.

Like the new-born sun's that strikes the dark and
    slays it,
  So that even for love of light it smiles and dies,
Laughs the boy's blithe face whose fair fourth year
    arrays it
All with light of life and mirth that stirs and sways it
  And fulfils the deep wide eyes.

Wide and warm with glowing laughter's exultation,
Full of welcome, full of sunbright jubilation,
  Flash my taller friend's quick eyebeams, charged
    with glee ;
But with softer still and sweeter salutation
  Shine my smaller friend's on me.

Little arms flung round my bending neck, that yoke it
  Fast in tender bondage, draw my face down too
Toward the flower-soft face whose dumb deep smiles
    invoke it ;
Dumb, but love can read the radiant eyes that
    woke it,
  Blue as June's mid heaven is blue.

How may men find refuge, how should hearts be
    shielded,
From the weapons thus by little children wielded,
  When they lift such eyes as light this lustrous face—
Eyes that woke love sleeping unawares, and yielded
  Love for love, a gift of grace,

Grace beyond man's merit, love that laughs, forgiving
  Even the sin of being no more a child, nor worth
Trust and love that lavish gifts above man's giving,
Touch or glance of eyes and lips the sweetest living,
  Fair as heaven and kind as earth ?

NIGHT

I

FROM THE ITALIAN OF GIOVANNI STROZZI

Night, whom in shape so sweet thou here may'st see
  Sleeping, was by an Angel sculptured thus
  In marble, and since she sleeps hath life like us :
Thou doubt'st? Awake her : she will speak to thee.

II

FROM THE ITALIAN OF MICHELANGELO BUONARROTI

Sleep likes me well, and better yet to know
  I am but stone.   While shame and grief must be,
  Good hap is mine, to feel not, nor to see :
Take heed, then, lest thou wake me : ah, speak low.

IN TIME OF MOURNING

" RETURN," we dare not as we fain
 Would cry from hearts that yearn :
Love dares not bid our dead again
 Return.

 O hearts that strain and burn
As fires fast fettered burn and strain !
 Bow down, lie still, and learn.

The heart that healed all hearts of pain
 No funeral rites inurn :
Its echoes, while the stars remain,
 Return.

May 1885.

THE INTERPRETERS

I

DAYS dawn on us that make amends for many
      Sometimes,
When heaven and earth seem sweeter even than any
      Man's rhymes.

Light had not all been quenched in France, or
    quelled
      In Greece,
Had Homer sung not, or had Hugo held
      His peace.

Had Sappho's self not left her word thus long
      For token,
The sea round Lesbos yet in waves of song
      Had spoken.

II

And yet these days of subtler air and finer
      Delight,
When lovelier looks the darkness, and diviner
      The light—

The gift they give of all these golden hours,
      Whose urn
Pours forth reverberate rays or shadowing showers
      In turn—

Clouds, beams, and winds that make the live day's
    track
      Seem living—
What were they did no spirit give them back
      Thanksgiving?

III

Dead air, dead fire, dead shapes and shadows, telling
      Time nought;
Man gives them sense and soul by song, and dwelling
      In thought.

In human thought their being endures, their power
      Abides:
Else were their life a thing that each light hour
      Derides.

The years live, work, sigh, smile, and die, with all
      They cherish;
The soul endures, though dreams that fed it fall
      And perish.

IV

In human thought have all things habitation;
      Our days
Laugh, lower, and lighten past, and find no station
      That stays.

But thought and faith are mightier things than time
          Can wrong,
Made splendid once with speech, or made sublime
          By song.

Remembrance, though the tide of change that rolls
          Wax hoary,
Gives earth and heaven, for song's   sake and the
     soul's,
          Their glory.

July 16, 1885.

THE RECALL

RETURN, they cry, ere yet your day
  Set, and the sky grow stern :
Return, strayed souls, while yet ye may
  Return.

  But heavens beyond us yearn ;
Yea, heights of heaven above the sway
  Of stars that eyes discern.

The soul whose wings from shoreward stray
  Makes toward her viewless bourne
Though trustless faith and unfaith say,
  Return.

BY TWILIGHT

If we dream that desire of the distance above us
Should be fettered by fear of the shadows that seem,
If we wake, to be nought, but to hate or to love us
      If we dream,

Night sinks on the soul, and the stars as they gleam
Speak menace or mourning, with tongues to reprove
  us
That we deemed of them better than terror may
  deem.

But if hope may not lure us, if fear may not move
  us,
Thought lightens the darkness wherein the supreme
Pure presence of death shall assure us, and prove us
      If we dream.

A BABY'S EPITAPH

APRIL made me : winter laid me here away asleep.
Bright as Maytime was my daytime ; night is soft
and deep :
Though the morrow bring forth sorrow, well are ye
that weep.

Ye that held me dear beheld me not a twelvemonth
long :
All the while ye saw me smile, ye knew not whence
the song
Came that made me smile, and laid me here, and
wrought you wrong.

Angels, calling from your brawling world one undefiled,
Homeward bade me, and forbade me here to rest
beguiled :
Here I sleep not : pass, and weep not here upon
your child.

ON THE DEATH OF SIR HENRY TAYLOR

FOURSCORE and five times has the gradual year
   Risen and fulfilled its days of youth and eld
   Since first the child's eyes opening first beheld
Light, who now leaves behind to help us here
Light shed from song as starlight from a sphere
   Serene as summer ; song whose charm compelled
   The sovereign soul made flesh in Artevelde
To stand august before us and austere,
Half sad with mortal knowledge, all sublime
With trust that takes no taint from change or time,
Trust in man's might of manhood.   Strong and sage,
   Clothed round with reverence of remembering
      hearts,
He, twin-born with our nigh departing age,
   Into the light of peace and fame departs.

IN MEMORY OF JOHN WILLIAM INCHBOLD

FAREWELL : how should not such as thou fare well,
  Though we fare ill that love thee, and that live,
And know, whate'er the days wherein we dwell
  May give us, thee again they will not give ?

Peace, rest, and sleep are all we know of death,
  And all we dream of comfort : yet for thee,
Whose breath of life was bright and strenuous
    breath,
  We think the change is other than we see.

The seal of sleep set on thine eyes to-day
  Surely can seal not up the keen swift light
That lit them once for ever. Night can slay
  None save the children of the womb of night.

The fire that burns up dawn to bring forth noon
  Was father of thy spirit : how shouldst thou
Die as they die for whom the sun and moon
  Are silent ? Thee the darkness holds not now :

Them, while they looked upon the light, and
    deemed
  That life was theirs for living in the sun,
The darkness held in bondage : and they dreamed,
  Who knew not that such life as theirs was none.

To thee the sun spake, and the morning sang
  Notes deep and clear as life or heaven : the sea
That sounds for them but wild waste music rang
  Notes that were lost not when they rang for thee.

The mountains clothed with light and night and
    change,
  The lakes alive with wind and cloud and sun,
Made answer, by constraint sublime and strange,
  To the ardent hand that bade thy will be done.

We may not bid the mountains mourn, the sea
  That lived and lightened from thine hand again
Moan, as of old would men that mourned as we
  A man beloved, a man elect of men,

A man that loved them.   Vain, divine and vain,
  The dream that touched with thoughts or tears
    of ours
The spirit of sense that lives in sun and rain,
  Sings out in birds, and breathes and fades in
    flowers.

Not for our joy they live, and for our grief
  They die not.   Though thine eye be closed,
    thine hand
Powerless as mine to paint them, not a leaf
  In English woods or glades of Switzerland

Falls earlier now, fades faster.   All our love
  Moves not our mother's changeless heart, who
    gives
A little light to eyes and stars above,
  A little life to each man's heart that lives.

A little life to heaven and earth and sea,
    To stars and souls revealed of night and day,
And change, the one thing changeless : yet shall she
    Cease too, perchance, and perish.   Who shall say ?

Our mother Nature, dark and sweet as sleep,
    And strange as life and strong as death, holds fast,
Even as she holds our hearts alive, the deep
    Dumb secret of her first-born births and last.

But this, we know, shall cease not till the strife
    Of nights and days and fears and hopes find end ;
This, through the brief eternities of life,
    Endures, and calls from death a living friend ;

The love made strong with knowledge, whence con-
    firmed
    The whole soul takes assurance, and the past
(So by time's measure, not by memory's, termed)
    Lives present life, and mingles first with last.

I, now long since thy guest of many days,
    Who found thy hearth a brother's, and with thee
Tracked in and out the lines of rolling bays
    And banks and gulfs and reaches of the sea—

Deep dens wherein the wrestling water sobs
    And pants with restless pain of refluent breath
Till all the sunless hollow sounds and throbs
    With ebb and flow of eddies dark as death—

I know not what more glorious world, what waves
    More bright with life,—if brighter aught may live
Than those that filled and fled their tidal caves—
    May now give back the love thou hast to give.

Tintagel, and the long Trebarwith sand,
  Lone Camelford, and Boscastle divine
With dower of southern blossom, bright and bland
  Above the roar of granite-baffled brine,

Shall hear no more by joyous night or day
  From downs or causeways good to rove and ride
Or feet of ours or horse-hoofs urge their way
  That sped us here and there by tower and tide.

The headlands and the hollows and the waves,
  For all our love, forget us : where I am
Thou art not : deeper sleeps the shadow on graves
  Than in the sunless gulf that once we swam.

Thou hast swum too soon the sea of death : for us
  Too soon, but if truth bless love's blind belief
Faith, born of hope and memory, says not thus :
  And joy for thee for me should mean not grief.

And joy for thee, if ever soul of man
  Found joy in change and life of ampler birth
Than here pens in the spirit for a span,
  Must be the life that doubt calls death on earth.

For if, beyond the shadow and the sleep,
  A place there be for souls without a stain,
Where peace is perfect, and delight more deep
  Than seas or skies that change and shine again,

There none of all unsullied souls that live
  May hold a surer station : none may lend
More light to hope's or memory's lamp, nor give
  More joy than thine to those that called thee friend.

Yea, joy from sorrow's barren womb is born
  When faith begets on grief the godlike child :
As midnight yearns with starry sense of morn
  In Arctic summers, though the sea wax wild,

So love, whose name is memory, thrills at heart,
  Remembering and rejoicing in thee, now
Alive where love may dream not what thou art
  But knows that higher than hope or love art thou.

" Whatever heaven, if heaven at all may be,
  Await the sacred souls of good men dead,
There, now we mourn who loved him here, is he."
  So, sweet and stern of speech, the Roman said,

Erect in grief, in trust erect, and gave
  His deathless dead a deathless life even here
Where day bears down on day as wave on wave
  And not man's smile fades faster than his tear.

Albeit this gift be given not me to give,
  Nor power be mine to break time's silent spell,
Not less shall love that dies not while I live
  Bid thee, beloved in life and death, farewell.

NEW YEAR'S DAY

NEW YEAR, be good to England. Bid her name
  Shine sunlike as of old on all the sea :
  Make strong her soul : set all her spirit free :
Bind fast her homeborn foes with links of shame
More strong than iron and more keen than flame :
  Seal up their lips for shame's sake : so shall she
  Who was the light that lightened freedom be,
For all false tongues, in all men's eyes the same.

O last-born child of Time, earth's eldest lord,
  God undiscrowned of godhead, who for man
    Begets all good and evil things that live,
Do thou, his new-begotten son, implored
  Of hearts that hope and fear not, make thy span
    Bright with such light as history bids thee give.

Jan. 1, 1889.

TO SIR RICHARD F. BURTON

(ON HIS TRANSLATION OF "THE ARABIAN NIGHTS")

WESTWARD the sun sinks, grave and glad ; but far
  Eastward, with laughter and tempestuous tears,
  Cloud, rain, and splendour as of orient spears,
Keen as the sea's thrill toward a kindling star,
The sundawn breaks the barren twilight's bar
  And fires the mist and slays it.   Years on years
  Vanish, but he that hearkens eastward hears
Bright music from the world where shadows are.

Where shadows are not shadows.   Hand in hand
A man's word bids them rise and smile and stand
  And triumph.   All that glorious orient glows
Defiant of the dusk.   Our twilight land
  Trembles ; but all the heaven is all one rose,
  Whence laughing love dissolves her frosts and
    snows.

NELL GWYN

SWEET heart, that no taint of the throne or the stage
  Could touch with unclean transformation, or alter
   To the likeness of courtiers whose consciences
    falter
At the smile or the frown, at the mirth or the rage,
Of a master whom chance could inflame or assuage,
  Our Lady of Laughter, invoked in no psalter,
  Adored of no faithful that cringe and that palter,
Praise be with thee yet from a hag-ridden age.

Our Lady of Pity thou wast : and to thee
All England, whose sons are the sons of the sea,
  Gives thanks, and will hear not if history snarls
When the name of the friend of her sailors is spoken ;
And thy lover she cannot but love—by the token
  That thy name was the last on the lips of King
    Charles.

CALIBAN ON ARIEL

" His backward voice is to utter foul speeches and to detract"

THE tongue is loosed of that most lying slave,
   Whom stripes may move, not kindness. Listen:
     " Lo,
  The real god of song, Lord Stephano,
That's a brave god, if ever god were brave,
And bears celestial liquor: but," the knave
   (A most ridiculous monster) howls, " we know
   From Ariel's lips what springs of poison flow,
The chicken-heart blasphemer! Hear him rave!"

Thou poisonous slave, got by the devil himself
   Upon thy wicked dam, the witch whose name
    Is darkness, and the sun her eyes' offence,
Though hell's hot sewerage breed no loathlier elf,
   Men cry not shame upon thee, seeing thy shame
    So perfect: they but bid thee—" Hag-seed,
     hence!"

THE WEARY WEDDING

O DAUGHTER, why do ye laugh and weep,
    One with another ?
For woe to wake and for will to sleep,
    Mother, my mother.

But weep ye winna the day ye wed,
    One with another.
For tears are dry when the springs are dead,
    Mother, my mother.

Too long have your tears run down like rain,
    One with another.
For a long love lost and a sweet love slain,
    Mother, my mother.

Too long have your tears dripped down like dew,
    One with another.
For a knight that my sire and my brethren slew,
    Mother, my mother.

Let past things perish and dead griefs lie,
    One with another.
O fain would I weep not, and fain would I die,
    Mother, my mother.

Fair gifts we give ye, to laugh and live,
    One with another.
But sair and strange are the gifts I give,
    Mother, my mother.

And what will ye give for your father's love?
    One with another.
Fruits full few and thorns enough,
    Mother, my mother.

And what will ye give for your mother's sake?
    One with another.
Tears to brew and tares to bake,
    Mother, my mother.

And what will ye give your sister Jean?
    One with another.
A bier to build and a babe to wean,
    Mother, my mother.

And what will ye give your sister Nell?
    One with another.
The end of life and beginning of heil,
    Mother, my mother.

And what will ye give your sister Kate?
    One with another.
Earth's door and hell's gate,
    Mother, my mother.

And what will ye give your brother Will?
    One with another.
Life's grief and world's ill,
    Mother, my mother.

And what will ye give your brother Hugh?
    One with another.
A bed of turf to turn into,
    Mother, my mother.

And what will ye give your brother John?
    One with another.
The dust of death to feed upon,
    Mother, my mother.

And what will ye give your bauld bridegroom?
    One with another.
A barren bed and an empty room,
    Mother, my mother.

And what will ye give your bridegroom's friend?
    One with another.
A weary foot to the weary end,
    Mother, my mother.

And what will ye give your blithe bridesmaid?
    One with another.
Grief to sew and sorrow to braid,
    Mother, my mother.

And what will ye drink the day ye're wed?
    One with another.
But ae drink of the wan well-head,
    Mother, my mother.

And whatten a water is that to draw?
    One with another.
We maun draw thereof a', we maun drink there-
      of a',
    Mother, my mother.

And what shall ye pu' where the well rins deep?
    One with another.
Green herb of death, fine flower of sleep,
    Mother, my mother.

Are there ony fishes that swim therein?
    One with another.
The white fish grace, and the red fish sin,
    Mother, my mother.

Are there ony birds that sing thereby?
    One with another.
O when they come thither they sing till they die,
    Mother, my mother.

Is there ony draw-bucket to that well-head?
    One with another.
There's a wee well-bucket hangs low by a thread,
    Mother, my mother.

And whatten a thread is that to spin?
    One with another.
It's green for grace, and it's black for sin,
    Mother, my mother.

And what will ye strew on your bride-chamber
    floor?
    One with another.
But one strewing and no more,
    Mother, my mother.

And whatten a strewing shall that one be?
    One with another.
The dust of earth and sand of the sea,
    Mother my mother.

And what will ye take to build your bed?
  One with another.
Sighing and shame and the bones of the dead,
  Mother, my mother.

And what will ye wear for your wedding gown?
  One with another.
Grass for the green and dust for the brown
  Mother, my mother.

And what will ye wear for your wedding lace?
  One with another.
A heavy heart and a hidden face,
  Mother, my mother.

And what will ye wear for a wreath to your head?
  One with another.
Ash for the white and blood for the red,
  Mother, my mother.

And what will ye wear for your wedding ring?
  One with another.
A weary thought for a weary thing,
  Mother, my mother.

And what shall the chimes and the bell-ropes play?
  One with another.
A weary tune on a weary day,
  Mother, my mother.

And what shall be sung for your wedding song?
  One with another.
A weary word of a weary wrong,
  Mother, my mother.

The world's way with me runs back,
        One with another,
Wedded in white and buried in black,
        Mother, my mother.

The world's day and the world's night,
        One with another,
Wedded in black and buried in white,
        Mother, my mother.

The world's bliss and the world's teen,
        One with another,
It's red for white and it's black for green,
        Mother, my mother.

The world's will and the world's way,
        One with another,
It's sighing for night and crying for day,
        Mother, my mother.

The world's good and the world's worth,
        One with another,
It's earth to flesh and it's flesh to earth,
        Mother, my mother.

*   *   *   *   *   *

When she came out at the kirkyard gate,
        (One with another)
The bridegroom's mother was there in wait.
        (Mother, my mother.)

O mother, where is my great green bed,
        (One with another)
Silk at the foot and gold at the head,
        Mother, my mother?

Yea, it is ready, the silk and the gold,
　　One with another.
But line it well that I lie not cold,
　　Mother, my mother.

She laid her cheek to the velvet and vair,
　　One with another;
She laid her arms up under her hair.
　　(Mother, my mother.)

Her gold hair fell through her arms fu' low,
　　One with another:
Lord God, bring me out of woe!
　　(Mother, my mother.)

Her gold hair fell in the gay reeds green,
　　One with another:
Lord God, bring me out of teen!
　　(Mother, my mother.)

*　　*　　*　　*　　*　　*

O mother, where is my lady gone?
　　(One with another.)
In the bride-chamber she makes sore moan:
　　(Mother, my mother.)

Her hair falls over the velvet and vair,
　　(One with another)
Her great soft tears fall over her hair.
　　(Mother, my mother.)

When he came into the bride's chamber,
　　(One with another)
Her hands were like pale yellow amber.
　　(Mother, my mother.)

Her tears made specks in the velvet and vair,
	(One with another)
The seeds of the reeds made specks in her hair.
	(Mother, my mother.)

He kissed her under the gold on her head ;
	(One with another)
The lids of her eyes were like cold lead.
	(Mother, my mother.)

He kissed her under the fall of her chin ;
	(One with another)
There was right little blood therein.
	(Mother, my mother.)

He kissed her under her shoulder sweet ;
	(One with another)
Her throat was weak, with little heat.
	(Mother, my mother.)

He kissed her down by her breast-flowers red,
	One with another ;
They were like river-flowers dead.
	(Mother, my mother.)

What ails you now o' your weeping, wife ?
	(One with another.)
It ails me sair o' my very life.
	(Mother, my mother.)

What ails you now o' your weary ways ?
	(One with another.)
It ails me sair o' my long life-days.
	(Mother, my mother.)

Nay, ye are young, ye are over fair.
    (One with another.)
Though I be young, what needs ye care?
    (Mother, my mother.)

Nay, ye are fair, ye are over sweet.
    (One with another.)
Though I be fair, what needs ye greet?
    (Mother, my mother.)

Nay, ye are mine while I hold my life.
    (One with another.)
O fool, will ye marry the worm for a wife?
    (Mother, my mother.)

Nay, ye are mine while I have my breath.
    (One with another.)
O fool, will ye marry the dust of death?
    (Mother, my mother.)

Yea, ye are mine, we are handfast wed,
    One with another.
Nay, I am no man's; nay, I am dead,
    Mother, my mother.

THE WINDS

O WEARY fa' the east wind,
  And weary fa' the west :
And gin I were under the wan waves wide
  I wot weel wad I rest.

O weary fa' the north wind,
  And weary fa' the south :
The sea went ower my good lord's head
  Or ever he kissed my mouth.

Weary fa' the windward rocks,
  And weary fa' the lee :
They might hae sunken sevenscore ships,
  And let my love's gang free.

And weary fa' ye, mariners a',
  And weary fa' the sea :
It might hae taken an hundred men,
  And let my ae love be.

A LYKE-WAKE SONG

Fair of face, full of pride,
Sit ye down by a dead man's side.

Ye sang songs a' the day :
Sit down at night in the red worm's way.

Proud ye were a' day long :
Ye'll be but lean at evensong.

Ye had gowd kells on your hair :
Nae man kens what ye were.

Ye set scorn by the silken stuff :
Now the grave is clean enough.

Ye set scorn by the rubis ring :
Now the worm is a saft sweet thing.

Fine gold and blithe fair face,
Ye are come to a grimly place.

Gold hair and glad grey een,
Nae man kens if ye have been.

A REIVER'S NECK-VERSE

SOME die singing, and some die swinging,
  And weel mot a' they be :
Some die playing, and some die praying,
  And I wot sae winna we, my dear,
  And I wot sae winna we.

Some die sailing, and some die wailing,
  And some die fair and free :
Some die flyting, and some die fighting,
  But I for a fause love's fee, my dear,
  But I for a fause love's fee.

Some die laughing, and some die quaffing,
  And some die high on tree :
Some die spinning, and some die sinning,
  But faggot and fire for ye, my dear,
  Faggot and fire for ye.

Some die weeping, and some die sleeping,
  And some die under sea :
Some die ganging, and some die hanging,
  And a twine of a tow for me, my dear,
  A twine of a tow for me.

THE WITCH-MOTHER

"O WHERE will ye gang to and where will ye sleep,
    Against the night begins?"
"My bed is made wi' cauld sorrows,
    My sheets are lined wi' sins.

"And a sair grief sitting at my foot,
    And a sair grief at my head;
And dule to lay me my laigh pillows,
    And teen till I be dead.

"And the rain is sair upon my face,
    And sair upon my hair;
And the wind upon my weary mouth,
    That never may man kiss mair.

"And the snow upon my heavy lips,
    That never shall drink nor eat;
And shame to cledding, and woe to wedding,
    And pain to drink and meat.

"But woe be to my bairns' father,
    And ever ill fare he:
He has tane a braw bride hame to him,
    Cast out my bairns and me."

VOL. III.   T

" And what shall they have to their marriage meat
   This day they twain are wed?"
" Meat of strong crying, salt of sad sighing,
   And God restore the dead."

" And what shall they have to their wedding wine
   This day they twain are wed?"
" Wine of weeping, and draughts of sleeping,
   And God raise up the dead."

She's tane her to the wild woodside,
   Between the flood and fell:
She's sought a rede against her need
   Of the fiend that bides in hell.

She's tane her to the wan burnside,
   She's wrought wi' sang and spell:
She's plighted her soul for doom and doie
   To the fiend that bides in hell.

She's set her young son to her breast,
   Her auld son to her knee:
Says, " Weel for you the night, bairnies,
   And weel the morn for me."

She looked fu' lang in their een, sighing,
   And sair and sair grat she:
She has slain her young son at her breast,
   Her auld son at her knee.

She's sodden their flesh wi' saft water,
   She's mixed their blood with wine:
She's tane her to the braw bride-house,
   Where a' were boun' to dine.

She poured the red wine in his cup,
  And his een grew fain to greet :
She set the baked meats at his hand,
  And bade him drink and eat.

Says, " Eat your fill of your flesh, my lord,
  And drink your fill of your wine ;
For a' thing's yours and only yours
  That has been yours and mine."

Says, " Drink your fill of your wine, my lord,
  And eat your fill of your bread :
I would they were quick in my body again,
  Or I that bare them dead."

He struck her head frae her fair body,
  And dead for grief he fell :
And there were twae mair sangs in heaven,
  And twae mair sauls in hell.

THE BRIDE'S TRAGEDY

"The wind wears roun', the day wears doun,
  The moon is grisly grey;
There's nae man rides by the mirk muirsides,
  Nor down the dark Tyne's way."
    In, in, out and in,
    Blaws the wind and whirls the whin.

"And winna ye watch the night wi' me,
  And winna ye wake the morn?
Foul shame it were that your ae mither
  Should brook her ae son's scorn."
    In, in, out and in,
    Blaws the wind and whirls the whin.

"O mither, I may not sleep nor stay,
  My weird is ill to dree;
For a fause faint lord of the south seaboard
  Wad win my bride of me."
    In, in, out and in,
    Blaws the wind and whirls the whin.

"The winds are strang, and the nights are lang,
  And the ways are sair to ride:
And I maun gang to wreak my wrang,
  And ye maun bide and bide."
    In, in, out and in,
    Blaws the wind and whirls the whin.

" Gin I maun bide and bide, Willie,
   I wot my weird is sair :
Weel may ye get ye a light love yet,
   But never a mither mair."
      In, in, out and in,
      Blaws the wind and whirls the whin.

" O gin the morrow be great wi' sorrow,
   The wyte be yours of a' :
But though ye slay me that haud and stay me,
   The weird ye will maun fa'."
      In, in, out and in,
      Blaws the wind and whirls the whin.

When cocks were crawing and day was dawing,
   He's boun' him forth to ride :
And the ae first may he's met that day
   Was fause Earl Robert's bride.
      In, in, out and in,
      Blaws the wind and whirls the whin.

O blithe and braw were the bride-folk a',
   But sad and saft rade she ;
And sad as doom was her fause bridegroom,
   But fair and fain was he.
      In, in, out and in,
      Blaws the wind and whirls the whin.

" And winna ye bide, sae saft ye ride,
   And winna ye speak wi' me ?
For mony's the word and the kindly word
   I have spoken aft wi' thee."
      In, in, out and in,
      Blaws the wind and whirls the whin.

" My lamp was lit yestreen, Willie,
   My window-gate was wide :
But ye camena nigh me till day came by me
   And made me not your bride."
      In, in, out and in,
      Blaws the wind and whirls the whin.

He's set his hand to her bridle-rein,
   He's turned her horse away :
And the cry was sair, and the wrath was mair,
   And fast and fain rode they.
      In, in, out and in,
      Blaws the wind and whirls the whin.

But when they came by Chollerford,
   I wot the ways were fell ;
For broad and brown the spate swang down,
   And the lift was mirk as hell.
      In, in, out and in,
      Blaws the wind and whirls the whin.

"And will ye ride yon fell water,
   Or will ye bide for fear?
Nae scathe ye'll win o' your father s kin,
   Though they should slay me here."
      In, in, out and in,
      Blaws the wind and whirls the whin.

" I had liefer ride yon fell water,
   Though strange it be to ride,
Than I wad stand on the fair green strand
   And thou be slain beside."
      In, in, out and in,
      Blaws the wind and whirls the whin.

" I had liefer swim yon wild water,
   Though sair it be to bide,
Than I wad stand at a strange man's hand,
   To be a strange man's bride."
     In, in, out and in,
     Blaws the wind and whirls the whin.

" I had liefer drink yon dark water,
   Wi' the stanes to make my bed,
And the faem to hide me, and thou beside me,
   Than I wad see thee dead."
     In, in, out and in,
     Blaws the wind and whirls the whin.

He's kissed her twice, he's kissed her thrice,
   On cheek and lip and chin :
He's wound her rein to his hand again,
   And lightly they leapt in.
     In, in, out and in,
     Blaws the wind and whirls the whin.

Their hearts were high to live or die,
   Their steeds were stark of limb :
But the stream was starker, the spate was darker,
   Than man might live and swim.
     In, in, out and in,
     Blaws the wind and whirls the whin.

The first ae step they strode therein,
   It smote them foot and knee :
But ere they wan to the mid water
   The spate was as the sea.
     In, in, out and in,
     Blaws the wind and whirls the whin.

But when they wan to the mid water,
　　It smote them hand and head :
And nae man knows but the wave that flows
　　Where they lie drowned and dead.
　　　In, in, out and in,
　　　Blaws the wind and whirls the whin.

A JACOBITE'S FAREWELL

1716

THERE's nae mair lands to tyne, my dear,
    And nae mair lives to gie :
Though a man think sair to live nae mair,
    There's but one day to die.

For a' things come and a' days gane,
    What needs ye rend your hair ?
But kiss me till the morn's morrow,
    Then I'll kiss ye nae mair.

O lands are lost and life's losing,
    And what were they to gie ?
Fu' mony a man gives all he can,
    But nae man else gives ye.

Our king wons ower the sea's water,
    And I in prison sair :
But I'll win out the morn's morrow,
    And ye'll see me nae mair.

A JACOBITE'S EXILE

1746

THE weary day rins down and dies,
　The weary night wears through :
And never an hour is fair wi' flower,
　And never a flower wi' dew.

I would the day were night for me,
　I would the night were day :
For then would I stand in my ain fair land,
　As now in dreams I may.

O lordly flow the Loire and Seine,
　And loud the dark Durance :
But bonnier shine the braes of Tyne
　Than a' the fields of France ;
And the waves of Till that speak sae still
　Gleam goodlier where they glance.

O weel were they that fell fighting
　On dark Drumossie's day :
They keep their hame ayont the faem,
　And we die far away.

O sound they sleep, and saft, and deep,
  But night and day wake we ;
And ever between the sea-banks green
  Sounds loud the sundering sea.

And ill we sleep, sae sair we weep,
  But sweet and fast sleep they ;
And the mool that haps them roun' and laps them
  Is e'en their country's clay ;
But the land we tread that are not dead
  Is strange as night by day.

Strange as night in a strange man's sight,
  Though fair as dawn it be :
For what is here that a stranger's cheer
  Should yet wax blithe to see ?

The hills stand steep, the dells lie deep,
  The fields are green and gold :
The hill-streams sing, and the hill-sides ring,
  As ours at home of old.

But hills and flowers are nane of ours,
  And ours are oversea :
And the kind strange land whereon we stand,
  It wotsna what were we
Or ever we came, wi' scathe and shame,
  To try what end might be.

Scathe, and shame, and a waefu' name,
  And a weary time and strange,
Have they that seeing a weird for dreeing
  Can die, and cannot change.

Shame and scorn may we thole that mourn,
　　Though sair be they to dree :
But ill may we bide the thoughts we hide,
　　Mair keen than wind and sea.

Ill may we thole the night's watches,
　　And ill the weary day :
And the dreams that keep the gates of sleep,
　　A waefu' gift gie they ;
For the sangs they sing us, the sights they
　　　　bring us,
　　The morn blaws all away.

On Aikenshaw the sun blinks braw,
　　The burn rins blithe and fain :
There's nought wi' me I wadna gie
　　To look thereon again.

On Keilder-side the wind blaws wide ;
　　There sounds nae hunting-horn
That rings sae sweet as the winds that beat
　　Round banks where Tyne is born.

The Wansbeck sings with all her springs,
　　The bents and braes give ear ;
But the wood that rings wi' the sang she sings
　　I may not see nor hear ;
For far and far thae blithe burns are,
　　And strange is a' thing near.

The light there lightens, the day there brightens,
　　The loud wind there lives free :
Nae light comes nigh me or wind blaws by me
　　That I wad hear or see.

But O gin I were there again,
  Afar ayont the faem,
Cauld and dead in the sweet saft bed
  That haps my sires at hame !

We'll see nae mair the sea-banks fair,
  And the sweet grey gleaming sky,
And the lordly strand of Northumberland,
  And the goodly towers thereby :
And none shall know but the winds that blow
  The graves wherein we lie.

THE TYNESIDE WIDOW

THERE'S mony a man loves land and life,
  Loves life and land and fee ;
And mony a man loves fair women,
  But never a man loves me, my love,
  But never a man loves me.

O weel and weel for a' lovers,
  I wot weel may they be ;
And weel and weel for a' fair maidens,
  But aye mair woe for me, my love,
  But aye mair woe for me.

O weel be wi' you, ye sma' flowers,
  Ye flowers and every tree ;
And weel be wi' you, a' birdies,
  But teen and tears wi' me, my love,
  But teen and tears wi' me.

O weel be yours, my three brethren,
  And ever weel be ye ;
Wi' deeds for doing and loves for wooing,
  But never a love for me, my love,
  But never a love for me.

And weel be yours, my seven sisters,
  And good love-days to see,
And long life-days and true lovers,
  But never a day for me, my love,
  But never a day for me.

Good times wi' you, ye bauld riders,
  By the hieland and the lee ;
And by the leeland and by the hieland
  It's weary times wi' me, my love,
  It's weary times wi' me.

Good days wi' you, ye good sailors,
  Sail in and out the sea ;
And by the beaches and by the reaches
  It's heavy days wi' me, my love,
  It's heavy days wi' me.

I had his kiss upon my mouth,
  His bairn upon my knee ;
I would my soul and body were twain,
  And the bairn and the kiss wi' me, my love,
  And the bairn and the kiss wi' me.

The bairn down in the mools, my dear,
  O saft and saft lies she ;
I would the mools were ower my head,
  And the young bairn fast wi' me, my love,
  And the young bairn fast wi' me.

The father under the faem, my dear,
  O sound and sound sleeps he ;
I would the faem were ower my face,
  And the father lay by me, my love,
  And the father lay by me.

I would the faem were ower my face,
  Or the mools on my ee-bree ;
And waking-time with a' lovers,
  But sleeping-time wi' me, my love,
  But sleeping-time wi' me.

I would the mools were meat in my mouth,
  The saut faem in my ee ;
And the land-worm and the water-worm
  To feed fu' sweet on me, my love,
  To feed fu' sweet on me.

My life is sealed with a seal of love,
  And locked with love for a key ;
And I lie wrang and I wake lang,
  But ye tak' nae thought for me, my love,
  But ye tak' nae thought for me.

We were weel fain of love, my dear,
  O fain and fain were we ;
It was weel with a' the weary world,
  But O, sae weel wi' me, my love,
  But O, sae weel wi' me.

We were nane ower mony to sleep, my dear,
  I wot we were but three ;
And never a bed in the weary world
  For my bairn and my dear and me, my love,
  For my bairn and my dear and me.

DEDICATION

THE years are many, the changes more,
Since wind and sun on the wild sweet shore
  Where Joyous Gard stands stark by the sea
With face as bright as in years of yore

Shone, swept, and sounded, and laughed for glee
More deep than a man's or a child's may be,
  On a day when summer was wild and glad,
And the guests of the wind and the sun were we.

The light that lightens from seasons clad
With darkness now, is it glad or sad?
  Not sad but glad should it shine, meseems,
On eyes yet fain of the joy they had.

For joy was there with us ; joy that gleams
And murmurs yet in the world of dreams
  Where thought holds fast, as a constant warder,
The days when I rode by moors and streams,

Reining my rhymes into buoyant order
Through honied leagues of the northland border.
  Though thought or memory fade, and prove
A faithless keeper, a thriftless hoarder,

DEDICATION

TO EDWARD JOHN TRELAWNY

A SEA-MEW on a sea-king's wrist alighting,
  As the north sea-wind caught and strained and curled
The raven-figured flag that led men fighting
  From field to green field of the water-world,
Might find such brief high favour at his hand
  For wings imbrued with brine, with foam impearled,
As these my songs require at yours on land,
  That durst not save for love's free sake require,
Being lightly born between the foam and sand,
  But reared by hope and memory and desire
Of lives that were and life that is to be,
  Even such as filled his heavenlier song with fire
Whose very voice, that sang to set man free,
  Was in your ears as ever in ours his lyre,
Once, ere the flame received him from the sea.

THALASSIUS

UPON the flowery forefront of the year,
One wandering by the grey-green April sea
Found on a reach of shingle and shallower sand
Inlaid with starrier glimmering jewellery
Left for the sun's love and the light wind's cheer
Along the foam-flowered strand
Breeze-brightened, something nearer sea than land
Though the last shoreward blossom-fringe was near,
A babe asleep with flower-soft face that gleamed
To sun and seaward as it laughed and dreamed,
Too sure of either love for either's fear,
Albeit so birdlike slight and light, it seemed
Nor man nor mortal child of man, but fair
As even its twin-born tenderer spray-flowers were,
That the wind scatters like an Oread's hair.

For when July strewed fire on earth and sea
The last time ere that year,
Out of the flame of morn Cymothoe
Beheld one brighter than the sunbright sphere
Move toward her from its fieriest heart, whence trod
The live sun's very God,
Across the foam-bright water-ways that are
As heavenlier heavens with star for answering star,
And on her eyes and hair and maiden mouth
Felt a kiss falling fierier than the South

And heard above afar
A noise of songs and wind-enamoured wings
And lutes and lyres of milder and mightier strings,
And round the resonant radiance of his car
Where depth is one with height,
Light heard as music, music seen as light.
And with that second moondawn of the spring's
That fosters the first rose,
A sun-child whiter than the sunlit snows
Was born out of the world of sunless things
That round the round earth flows and ebbs and flows.

But he that found the sea-flower by the sea
And took to foster like a graft of earth
Was born of man's most highest and heavenliest birth,
Free-born as winds and stars and waves are free;
A warrior grey with glories more than years,
Though more of years than change the quick to dead
Had rained their light and darkness on his head;
A singer that in time's and memory's ears
Should leave such words to sing as all his peers
Might praise with hallowing heat of rapturous tears
Till all the days of human flight were fled.
And at his knees his fosterling was fed
Not with man's wine and bread
Nor mortal mother-milk of hopes and fears,
But food of deep memorial days long sped;
For bread with wisdom and with song for wine
Clear as the full calm's emerald hyaline.
And from his grave glad lips the boy would gather
Fine honey of song-notes goldener than gold,
More sweet than bees make of the breathing heather,
That he, as glad and bold,
Might drink as they, and keep his spirit from cold.
And the boy loved his laurel-laden hair

As his own father's risen on the eastern air,
And that less white brow-binding bayleaf bloom
More than all flowers his father's eyes relume ;
And those high songs he heard,
More than all notes of any landward bird,
More than all sounds less free
Than the wind's quiring to the choral sea.

High things the high song taught him ; how the breath
Too frail for life may be more strong than death ;
And this poor flash of sense in life, that gleams
As a ghost's glory in dreams,
More stabile than the world's own heart's root seems,
By that strong faith of lordliest love which gives
To death's own sightless-seeming eyes a light
Clearer, to death's bare bones a verier might,
Than shines or strikes from any man that lives.
How he that loves life overmuch shall die
The dog's death, utterly :
And he that much less loves it than he hates
All wrongdoing that is done
Anywhere always underneath the sun
Shall live a mightier life than time's or fate's.
One fairer thing he shewed him, and in might
More strong than day and night
Whose strengths build up time's towering period :
Yea, one thing stronger and more high than God,
Which if man had not, then should God not be :
And that was Liberty.
And gladly should man die to gain, he said,
Freedom ; and gladlier, having lost, lie dead.
For man's earth was not, nor the sweet sea-waves
His, nor his own land, nor its very graves,
Except they bred not, bore not, hid not slaves :

Into some new shape of a strange perfume
More potent than its light live spirit of bloom,
How shall not something of that soul relive,
That only soul that had such gifts to give
As lighten something even of all men's doom
Even from the labouring womb
Even to the seal set on the unopening tomb?
And these the loving light of song and love
Shall wrap and lap round and impend above,
Imperishable ; and all springs born illume
Their sleep with brighter thoughts than wake the dove
To music, when the hillside winds resume
The marriage-song of heather-flower and broom
And all the joy thereof.

    And hate the song too taught him : hate of all
That brings or holds in thrall
Of spirit or flesh, free-born ere God began,
The holy body and sacred soul of man.
And wheresoever a curse was or a chain,
A throne for torment or a crown for bane
Rose, moulded out of poor men's molten pain,
There, said he, should man's heaviest hate be set
Inexorably, to faint not or forget
Till the last warmth bled forth of the last vein
In flesh that none should call a king's again,
Seeing wolves and dogs and birds that plague-strike
    air
Leave the last bone of all the carrion bare.

    And hope the high song taught him : hope
      whose eyes
Can sound the seas unsoundable, the skies
Inaccessible of eyesight ; that can see

He felt the wind fitfully shift and heave
As toward a stormier eve ;
And all the wan wide sea shuddered ; and earth
Shook underfoot as toward some timeless birth,
Intolerable and inevitable ; and all
Heaven, darkling, trembled like a stricken thrall.
And far out of the quivering east, and far
From past the moonrise and its guiding star,
Began a noise of tempest and a light
That was not of the lightning ; and a sound
Rang with it round and round
That was not of the thunder ; and a flight
As of blown clouds by night,
That was not of them ; and with songs and cries
That sang and shrieked their soul out at the skies
A shapeless earthly storm of shapes began
From all ways round to move in on the man,
Clamorous against him silent ; and their feet
Were as the wind's are fleet,
And their shrill songs were as wild birds' are sweet.

And as when all the world of earth was wronged
And all the host of all men driven afoam
By the red hand of Rome,
Round some fierce amphitheatre overthronged
With fair clear faces full of bloodier lust
Than swells and stings the tiger when his mood
Is fieriest after blood
And drunk with trampling of the murderous must
That soaks and stains the tortuous close-coiled
    wood
Made monstrous with its myriad-mustering brood,
Face by fair face panted and gleamed and pressed,
And breast by passionate breast

Heaved hot with ravenous rapture, as they quaffed
The red ripe full fume of the deep live draught,
The sharp quick reek of keen fresh bloodshed, blown
Through the dense deep drift up to the emperor's
    throne
From the under steaming sands
With clamour of all-applausive throats and hands,
Mingling in mirthful time
With shrill blithe mockeries of the lithe-limbed mime :
So from somewhence far forth of the unbeholden,
Dreadfully driven from over and after and under,
Fierce, blown through fifes of brazen blast and
    golden,
With sound of chiming waves that drown the thunder
Or thunder that strikes dumb the sea's own chimes,
Began the bellowing of the bull-voiced mimes,
Terrible ; firs bowed down as briars or palms
Even at the breathless blast as of a breeze
Fulfilled with clamour and clangour and storms of
    psalms ;
Red hands rent up the roots of old-world trees,
Thick flames of torches tossed as tumbling seas
Made mad the moonless and infuriate air
That, ravening, revelled in the riotous hair
And raiment of the furred Bassarides.

    So came all those in on him ; and his heart,
As out of sleep suddenly struck astart,
Danced, and his flesh took fire of theirs, and grief
Was as a last year's leaf
Blown dead far down the wind's way ; and he set
His pale mouth to the brightest mouth it met
That laughed for love against his lips, and bade
Follow ; and in following all his blood grew glad

And as again a sea-bird's; for the wind
Took him to bathe him deep round breast and brow
Not as it takes a dead leaf drained and thinned,
But as the brightest bay-flower blown on bough,
Set springing toward it singing : and they rode
By many a vine-leafed, many a rose-hung road,
Exalt with exultation ; many a night
Set all its stars upon them as for spies
On many a moon-bewildering mountain-height
Where he rode only by the fierier light
Of his dread lady's hot sweet hungering eyes.
For the moon wandered witless of her way,
Spell-stricken by strong magic in such wise
As wizards use to set the stars astray.
And in his ears the music that makes mad
Beat always ; and what way the music bade,
That alway rode he ; nor was any sleep
His, nor from height nor deep.
But heaven was as red iron, slumberless,
And had no heart to bless ;
And earth lay sere and darkling as distraught,
And help in her was nought.

Then many a midnight, many a morn and even,
His mother, passing forth of her fair heaven,
With goodlier gifts than all save gods can give
From earth or from the heaven where sea-things live,
With shine of sea-flowers through the bay-leaf braid
Woven for a crown her foam-white hands had made
To crown him with land's laurel and sea-dew,
Sought the sea-bird that was her boy : but he
Sat panther-throned beside Erigone,
Riding the red ways of the revel through
Midmost of pale-mouthed passion's crownless crew.

Till on some winter's dawn of some dim year
He let the vine-bit on the panther's lip
Slide, and the green rein slip,
And set his eyes to seaward, nor gave ear
If sound from landward hailed him, dire or dear ;
And passing forth of all those fair fierce ranks
Back to the grey sea-banks,
Against a sea-rock lying, aslant the steep,
Fell after many sleepless dreams on sleep.

And in his sleep the dun green light was shed
Heavily round his head
That through the veil of sea falls fathom-deep,
Blurred like a lamp's that when the night drops dead
Dies ; and his eyes gat grace of sleep to see
The deep divine dark dayshine of the sea,
Dense water-walls and clear dusk water-ways,
Broad-based, or branching as a sea-flower sprays
That side or this dividing ; and anew
The glory of all her glories that he knew.
And in sharp rapture of recovering tears
He woke on fire with yearnings of old years,
Pure as one purged of pain that passion bore,
Ill child of bitter mother ; for his own
Looked laughing toward him from her midsea throne,
Up toward him there ashore.

Thence in his heart the great same joy began,
Of child that made him man :
And turned again from all hearts else on quest,
He communed with his own heart, and had rest.
And like sea-winds upon loud waters ran
His days and dreams together, till the joy
Burned in him of the boy.

Till the earth's great comfort and the sweet sea's
    breath
Breathed and blew life in where was heartless death,
Death spirit-stricken of soul-sick days, where strife
Of thought and flesh made mock of death and life.
And grace returned upon him of his birth
Where heaven was mixed with heavenlike sea and
    earth ;
And song shot forth strong wings that took the sun
From inward, fledged with might of sorrow and mirth
And father's fire made mortal in his son.
Nor was not spirit of strength in blast and breeze
To exalt again the sun's child and the sea's ;
For as wild mares in Thessaly grow great
With child of ravishing winds, that violate
Their leaping length of limb with manes like fire
And eyes outburning heaven's
With fires more violent than the lightning levin's
And breath drained out and desperate of desire,
Even so the spirit in him, when winds grew strong,
Grew great with child of song.
Nor less than when his veins first leapt for joy
To draw delight in such as burns a boy,
Now too the soul of all his senses felt
The passionate pride of deep sea-pulses dealt
Through nerve and jubilant vein
As from the love and largess of old time,
And with his heart again
The tidal throb of all the tides keep rhyme
And charm him from his own soul's separate sense
With infinite and invasive influence
That made strength sweet in him and sweetness
    strong,
Being now no more a singer, but a song.

Till one clear day when brighter sea-wind blew
And louder sea-shine lightened, for the waves
Were full of godhead and the light that saves,
His father's, and their spirit had pierced him through,
He felt strange breath and light all round him shed
That bowed him down with rapture ; and he knew
His father's hand, hallowing his humbled head,
And the old great voice of the old good time, that
    said :

" Child of my sunlight and the sea, from birth
A fosterling and fugitive on earth ;
Sleepless of soul as wind or wave or fire,
A manchild with an ungrown God's desire ;
Because thou hast loved nought mortal more than me,
Thy father, and thy mother-hearted sea ;
Because thou hast set thine heart to sing, and sold
Life and life's love for song, God's living gold ;
Because thou hast given thy flower and fire of youth
To feed men's hearts with visions, truer than truth ;
Because thou hast kept in those world-wandering eyes
The light that makes me music of the skies ;
Because thou hast heard with world-unwearied ears
The music that puts light into the spheres ;
Have therefore in thine heart and in thy mouth
The sound of song that mingles north and south,
The song of all the winds that sing of me,
And in thy soul the sense of all the sea."

ON THE CLIFFS

ἱμερόφωνος ἀηδών.

SAPPHO.

BETWEEN the moondawn and the sundown here
The twilight hangs half starless ; half the sea
Still quivers as for love or pain or fear
Or pleasure mightier than these all may be
A man's live heart might beat
Wherein a God's with mortal blood should meet
And fill its pulse too full to bear the strain
With fear or love or pleasure's twin-born, pain.
Fiercely the gaunt woods to the grim soil cling
That bears for all fair fruits
Wan wild sparse flowers of windy and wintry spring
Between the tortive serpent-shapen roots
Wherethrough their dim growth hardly strikes and
    shoots
And shews one gracious thing
Hardly, to speak for summer one sweet word
Of summer's self scarce heard.
But higher the steep green sterile fields, thick-set
With flowerless hawthorn even to the upward verge
Whence the woods gathering watch new cliffs emerge
Higher than their highest of crowns that sea-winds
    fret,

Hold fast, for all that night or wind can say,
Some pale pure colour yet,
Too dim for green and luminous for grey.
Between the climbing inland cliffs above
And these beneath that breast and break the bay,
A barren peace too soft for hate or love
Broods on an hour too dim for night or day.

O wind, O wingless wind that walk'st the sea,
Weak wind, wing-broken, wearier wind than we,
Who are yet not spirit-broken, maimed like thee,
Who wail not in our inward night as thou
In the outer darkness now,
What word has the old sea given thee for mine ear
From thy faint lips to hear ?
For some word would she send me, knowing not how.

Nay, what far other word
Than ever of her was spoken, or of me
Or all my winged white kinsfolk of the sea
Between fresh wave and wave was ever heard,
Cleaves the clear dark enwinding tree with tree
Too close for stars to separate and to see
Enmeshed in multitudinous unity ?
What voice of what strong God hath stormed and
    stirred
The fortressed rock of silence, rent apart
Even to the core Night's all-maternal heart ?
What voice of God grown heavenlier in a bird,
Made keener of edge to smite
Than lightning—yea, thou knowest, O mother Night,
Keen as that cry from thy strange children sent
Wherewith the Athenian judgment-shrine was rent,
For wrath that all their wrath was vainly spent,

Their wrath for wrong made right
By justice in her own divine despite
That bade pass forth unblamed
The sinless matricide and unashamed ?
Yea, what new cry is this, what note more bright
Than their song's wing of words was dark of flight,
What word is this thou hast heard,
Thine and not thine or theirs, O Night, what word
More keen than lightning and more sweet than light ?
As all men's hearts grew godlike in one bird
And all those hearts cried on thee, crying with might,
Hear us, O mother Night.

Dumb is the mouth of darkness as of death :
Light, sound and life are one
In the eyes and lips of dawn that draw the sun
To hear what first child's word with glimmering
    breath
Their weak wan weanling child the twilight saith ;
But night makes answer none.

God, if thou be God,—bird, if bird thou be,—
Do thou then answer me.
For but one word, what wind soever blow,
Is blown up usward ever from the sea.
In fruitless years of youth dead long ago
And deep beneath their own dead leaves and snow
Buried, I heard with bitter heart and sere
The same sea's word unchangeable, nor knew
But that mine own life-days were changeless too
And sharp and salt with unshed tear on tear
And cold and fierce and barren ; and my soul,
Sickening, swam weakly with bated breath
In a deep sea like death,

And felt the wind buffet her face with brine
Hard, and harsh thought on thought in long bleak
　　　roll
Blown by keen gusts of memory sad as thine
Heap the weight up of pain, and break, and leave
Strength scarce enough to grieve
In the sick heavy spirit, unmanned with strife
Of waves that beat at the tired lips of life.

Nay, sad may be man's memory, sad may be
The dream he weaves him as for shadow of thee,
But scarce one breathing-space, one heartbeat long,
Wilt thou take shadow of sadness on thy song.
Not thou, being more than man or man's desire,
Being bird and God in one,
With throat of gold and spirit of the sun ;
The sun whom all our souls and songs call sire,
Whose godhead gave thee, chosen of all our quire,
Thee only of all that serve, of all that sing
Before our sire and king,
Borne up some space on time's world-wandering
　　　wing,
This gift, this doom, to bear till time's wing tire—
Life everlasting of eternal fire.

Thee only of all ; yet can no memory say
How many a night and day
My heart has been as thy heart, and my life
As thy life is, a sleepless hidden thing,
Full of the thirst and hunger of winter and spring,
That seeks its food not in such love or strife
As fill men's hearts with passionate hours and rest.
From no loved lips and on no loving breast
Have I sought ever for such gifts as bring

Comfort, to stay the secret soul with sleep.
The joys, the loves, the labours, whence men reap
Rathe fruit of hopes and fears,
I have made not mine ; the best of all my days
Have been as those fair fruitless summer strays,
Those water-waifs that but the sea-wind steers,
Flakes of glad foam or flowers on footless ways
That take the wind in season and the sun,
And when the wind wills is their season done.

For all my days as all thy days from birth
My heart as thy heart was in me as thee,
Fire ; and not all the fountains of the sea
Have waves enough to quench it, nor on earth
Is fuel enough to feed,
While day sows night and night sows day for seed.

We were not marked for sorrow, thou nor I,
For joy nor sorrow, sister, were we made,
To take delight and grief to live and die,
Assuaged by pleasures or by pains affrayed
That melt men's hearts and alter ; we retain
A memory mastering pleasure and all pain,
A spirit within the sense of ear and eye,
A soul behind the soul, that seeks and sings
And makes our life move only with its wings
And feed but from its lips, that in return
Feed of our hearts wherein the old fires that burn
Have strength not to consume
Nor glory enough to exalt us past our doom.

Ah, ah, the doom (thou knowest whence rang that
      wail)
Of the shrill nightingale !

(From whose wild lips, thou knowest, that wail was
　　thrown)
For round about her have the great gods cast
A wing-borne body, and clothed her close and fast
With a sweet life that hath no part in moan.
But me, for me (how hadst thou heart to hear ?)
Remains a sundering with the two-edged spear.

Ah, for her doom! so cried in presage then
The bodeful bondslave of the king of men,
And might not win her will.
Too close the entangling dragnet woven of crime,
The snare of ill new-born of elder ill,
The curse of new time for an elder time,
Had caught, and held her yet,
Enmeshed intolerably in the intolerant net,
Who thought with craft to mock the God most high,
And win by wiles his crown of prophecy
From the Sun's hand sublime,
As God were man, to spare or to forget.

But thou,—the gods have given thee and forgiven thee
More than our master gave
That strange-eyed spirit-wounded strange-tongued
　　slave
There questing houndlike where the roofs red-wet
Reeked as a wet red grave.
Life everlasting has their strange grace given thee,
Even hers whom thou wast wont to sing and serve
With eyes, but not with song, too swift to swerve ;
Yet might not even thine eyes estranged estrange her,
Who seeing thee too, but inly, burn and bleed
Like that pale princess-priest of Priam's seed,
For stranger service gave thee guerdon stranger ;

If this indeed be guerdon, this indeed
Her mercy, this thy meed—
That thou, being more than all we born, being higher
Than all heads crowned of him that only gives
The light whereby man lives,
The bay that bids man moved of God's desire
Lay hand on lute or lyre,
Set lip to trumpet or deflowered green reed—
If this were given thee for a grace indeed,
That thou, being first of all these, thou alone
Shouldst have the grace to die not, but to live
And lose nor change one pulse of song, one tone
Of all that were thy lady's and thine own,
Thy lady's whom thou criedst on to forgive,
Thou, priest and sacrifice on the altar-stone
Where none may worship not of all that live,
Love's priestess, errant on dark ways diverse ;
If this were grace indeed for Love to give,
If this indeed were blessing and no curse.

Love's priestess, mad with pain and joy of song,
Song's priestess, mad with joy and pain of love,
Name above all names that are lights above,
We have loved, praised, pitied, crowned and done
    thee wrong,
O thou past praise and pity ; thou the sole
Utterly deathless, perfect only and whole
Immortal, body and soul.
For over all whom time hath overpast
The shadow of sleep inexorable is cast,
The implacable sweet shadow of perfect sleep
That gives not back what life gives death to keep ;
Yea, all that lived and loved and sang and sinned
Are all borne down death's cold sweet soundless wind

That blows all night and knows not whom its breath,
Darkling, may touch to death :
But one that wind hath touched and changed not,—
    one
Whose body and soul are parcel of the sun ;
One that earth's fire could burn not, nor the sea
Quench ; nor might human doom take hold on thee ;
All praise, all pity, all dreams have done thee wrong,
All love, with eyes love-blinded from above ;
Song's priestess, mad with joy and pain of love,
Love's priestess, mad with pain and joy of song.

Hast thou none other answer then for me
    Than the air may have of thee,
Or the earth's warm woodlands girdling with green
    girth
Thy secret sleepless burning life on earth,
Or even the sea that once, being woman crowned
And girt with fire and glory of anguish round,
Thou wert so fain to seek to, fain to crave
    If she would hear thee and save
And give thee comfort of thy great green grave?
Because I have known thee always who thou art,
Thou knowest, have known thee to thy heart's own
    heart,
Nor ever have given light ear to storied song
That did thy sweet name sweet unwitting wrong,
Nor ever have called thee nor would call for shame,
Thou knowest, but inly by thine only name,
Sappho—because I have known thee and loved, hast
    thou
None other answer now?
As brother and sister were we, child and bird,
Since thy first Lesbian word

Flamed on me, and I knew not whence I knew
This was the song that struck my whole soul through,
Pierced my keen spirit of sense with edge more keen,
Even when I knew not,—even ere sooth was seen,—
When thou wast but the tawny sweet winged thing
Whose cry was but of spring.

And yet even so thine ear should hear me—yea,
Hear me this nightfall by this northland bay,
Even for their sake whose loud good word I had,
Singing of thee in the all-beloved clime
Once, where the windy wine of spring makes mad
Our sisters of Majano, who kept time
Clear to my choral rhyme.
Yet was the song acclaimed of these aloud
Whose praise had made mute humbleness misproud,
The song with answering song applauded thus,
But of that Daulian dream of Itylus.
So but for love's love haply was it—nay,
How else?—that even their song took my song's part,
For love of love and sweetness of sweet heart,
Or god-given glorious madness of mid May
And heat of heart and hunger and thirst to sing,
Full of the new wine of the wind of spring.

Or if this were not, and it be not sin
To hold myself in spirit of thy sweet kin,
In heart and spirit of song ;
If this my great love do thy grace no wrong,
Thy grace that gave me grace to dwell therein ;
If thy gods thus be my gods, and their will
Made my song part of thy song—even such part
As man's hath of God's heart—
And my life like as thy life to fulfil ;

What have our gods then given us ?   Ah, to thee,
Sister, much more, much happier than to me,
Much happier things they have given, and more of
    grace
Than falls to man's light race ;
For lighter are we, all our love and pain
Lighter than thine, who knowest of time or place
Thus much, that place nor time
Can heal or hurt or lull or change again
The singing soul that makes his soul sublime
Who hears the far fall of its fire-fledged rhyme
Fill darkness as with bright and burning rain
Till all the live gloom inly glows, and light
Seems with the sound to cleave the core of night.

The singing soul that moves thee, and that moved
When thou wast woman, and their songs divine
Who mixed for Grecian mouths heaven's lyric wine
Fell dumb, fell down reproved
Before one sovereign Lesbian song of thine.
That soul, though love and life had fain held fast,
Wind-winged with fiery music, rose and past
Through the indrawn hollow of earth and heaven and
    hell,
As through some strait sea-shell
The wide sea's immemorial song,—the sea
That sings and breathes in strange men's ears of thee
How in her barren bride-bed, void and vast,
Even thy soul sang itself to sleep at last.

To sleep ?   Ah, then, what song is this, that here
Makes all the night one ear,
One ear fulfilled and mad with music, one
Heart kindling as the heart of heaven, to hear
A song more fiery than the awakening sun

Sings, when his song sets fire
To the air and clouds that build the dead night's
    pyre?
O thou of divers-coloured mind, O thou
Deathless, God's daughter subtle-souled—lo, now,
Now too the song above all songs, in flight
Higher than the day-star's height,
And sweet as sound the moving wings of night!
Thou of the divers-coloured seat—behold,
Her very song of old!—
O deathless, O God's daughter subtle-souled!
That same cry through this boskage overhead
Rings round reiterated,
Palpitates as the last palpitated,
The last that panted through her lips and died
Not down this grey north sea's half sapped cliff-side
That crumbles toward the coastline, year by year
More near the sands and near;
The last loud lyric fiery cry she cried,
Heard once on heights Leucadian,—heard not here.

Not here; for this that fires our northland night,
This is the song that made
Love fearful, even the heart of love afraid,
With the great anguish of its great delight.
No swan-song, no far-fluttering half-drawn breath,
No word that love of love's sweet nature saith,
No dirge that lulls the narrowing lids of death,
No healing hymn of peace-prevented strife,—
This is her song of life.

I loved thee,—hark, one tenderer note than all—
Atthis, of old time, once—one low long fall,
Sighing—one long low lovely loveless call,

Dying—one pause in song so flamelike fast—
Atthis, long since in old time overpast—
One soft first pause and last.
One,—then the old rage of rapture's fieriest rain
Storms all the music-maddened night again.

Child of God, close craftswoman, I beseech thee,
Bid not ache nor agony break nor master,
Lady, my spirit—
O thou her mistress, might her cry not reach thee?
Our Lady of all men's loves, could Love go past her,
Pass, and not hear it?

She hears not as she heard not; hears not me,
O treble-natured mystery,—how should she
Hear, or give ear?—who heard and heard not thee;
Heard, and went past, and heard not; but all time
Hears all that all the ravin of his years
Hath cast not wholly out of all men's ears
And dulled to death with deep dense funeral chime
Of their reiterate rhyme.
And now of all songs uttering all her praise,
All hers who had thy praise and did thee wrong,
Abides one song yet of her lyric days,
Thine only, this thy song.

O soul triune, woman and god and bird,
Man, man at least has heard.
All ages call thee conqueror, and thy cry
The mightiest as the least beneath the sky
Whose heart was ever set to song, or stirred
With wind of mounting music blown more high
Than wildest wing may fly,
Hath heard or hears,—even Æschylus as I.

But when thy name was woman, and thy word
Human,—then haply, surely then meseems
This thy bird's note was heard on earth of none,
Of none save only in dreams.
In all the world then surely was but one
Song; as in heaven at highest one sceptred sun
Regent, on earth here surely without fail
One only, one imperious nightingale.
Dumb was the field, the woodland mute, the lawn
Silent; the hill was tongueless as the vale
Even when the last fair waif of cloud that felt
Its heart beneath the colouring moonrays melt,
At high midnoon of midnight half withdrawn,
Bared all the sudden deep divine moondawn.
Then, unsaluted by her twin-born tune,
That latter timeless morning of the moon
Rose past its hour of moonrise; clouds gave way
To the old reconquering ray,
But no song answering made it more than day;
No cry of song by night
Shot fire into the cloud-constraining light.
One only, one Æolian island heard
Thrill, but through no bird's throat,
In one strange manlike maiden's godlike note,
The song of all these as a single bird.
Till the sea's portal was as funeral gate
For that sole singer in all time's ageless date
Singled and signed for so triumphal fate,
All nightingales but one in all the world
All her sweet life were silent; only then,
When her life's wing of womanhood was furled,
Their cry, this cry of thine was heard again,
As of me now, of any born of men.

Through sleepless clear spring nights filled full of
    thee,
Rekindled here, thy ruling song has thrilled
The deep dark air and subtle tender sea
And breathless hearts with one bright sound fulfilled.
Or at midnoon to me
Swimming, and birds about my happier head
Skimming, one smooth soft way by water and air,
To these my bright born brethren and to me
Hath not the clear wind borne or seemed to bear
A song wherein all earth and heaven and sea
Were molten in one music made of thee
To enforce us, O our sister of the shore,
Look once in heart back landward and adore?
For songless were we sea-mews, yet had we
More joy than all things joyful of thee—more,
Haply, than all things happiest ; nay, save thee,
In thy strong rapture of imperious joy
Too high for heart of sea-borne bird or boy,
What living things were happiest if not we?
But knowing not love nor change nor wrath nor
    wrong,
No more we knew of song.

Song, and the secrets of it, and their might,
What blessings curse it and what curses bless,
I know them since my spirit had first in sight,
Clear as thy song's words or the live sun's light,
The small dark body's Lesbian loveliness
That held the fire eternal ; eye and ear
Were as a god's to see, a god's to hear,
Through all his hours of daily and nightly chime,
The sundering of the two-edged spear of time :

The spear that pierces even the sevenfold shields
Of mightiest Memory, mother of all songs made,
And wastes all songs as roseleaves kissed and frayed
As here the harvest of the foam-flowered fields ;
But thine the spear may waste not that he wields
Since first the God whose soul is man's live breath,
The sun whose face hath our sun's face for shade,
Put all the light of life and love and death
Too strong for life, but not for love too strong,
Where pain makes peace with pleasure in thy song,
And in thine heart, where love and song make strife,
Fire everlasting of eternal life.

THE GARDEN OF CYMODOCE

SEA, and bright wind, and heaven of ardent air,
More dear than all things earth-born ; O to me
Mother more dear than love's own longing, sea,
More than love's eyes are, fair,
Be with my spirit of song as wings to bear,
As fire to feel and breathe and brighten ; be
A spirit of sense more deep of deity,
A light of love, if love may be, more strong
In me than very song.
For song I have loved with second love, but thee,
Thee first, thee, mother ; ere my songs had breath,
That love of loves, whose bondage makes man free,
Was in me strong as death.
And seeing no slave may love thee, no, not one
That loves not freedom more,
And more for thy sake loves her, and for hers
Thee ; or that hates not, on whate'er thy shore
Or what thy wave soever, all things done
Of man beneath the sun
In his despite and thine, to cross and curse
Your light and song that as with lamp and verse
Guide safe the strength of our sphered universe,
Thy breath it was, thou knowest, and none but
    thine,
That taught me love of one thing more divine.

Ah, yet my youth was old   [*Str.* 1.
Its first years dead and cold
As last year's autumn's gold,
And all my spirit of singing sick and sad and sere,
Or ever I might behold
The fairest of thy fold
Engirt, enringed, enrolled,
In all thy flower-sweet flock of islands dear and near.

Yet in my heart I deemed   [*Str.* 2.
The fairest things, meseemed,
Truth, dreaming, ever dreamed,
Had made mine eyes already like a god's to see :
Of all sea-things that were
Clothed on with water and air,
That none could live more fair
Than thy sweet love long since had shown for love
to me.

I knew not, mother of mine,   [*Ant.* 1
That one birth more divine
Than all births else of thine
That hang like flowers or jewels on thy deep soft
breast
Was left for me to shine
Above thy girdling line
Of bright and breathing brine,
To take mine eyes with rapture and my sense with
rest.

That this was left for me,   [*Ant.* 2.
Mother, to have of thee,
To touch, to taste, to see,
To feel as fire fulfilling all my blood and breath,

As wine of living fire
Keen as the heart's desire
That makes the heart its pyre
And on its burning visions burns itself to death.

For here of all thy waters, here of all
Thy windy ways the wildest, and beset
As some beleaguered city's war-breached wall
With deaths enmeshed all round it in deep net,
Thick sown with rocks deadlier than steel, and
        fierce
With loud cross-countering currents, where the
        ship
Flags, flickering like a wind-bewildered leaf,
The densest weft of waves that prow may pierce
Coils round the sharpest warp of shoals that dip
Suddenly, scarce well under for one brief
Keen breathing-space between the streams adverse,
Scarce showing the fanged edge of one hungering
        lip
Or one tooth lipless of the ravening reef;
And midmost of the murderous water's web
All round it stretched and spun,
Laughs, reckless of rough tide and raging ebb,
The loveliest thing that shines against the sun.

O flower of all wind-flowers and sea-flowers,   [*Str.* 3.
    Made lovelier by love of the sea
Than thy golden own field-flowers, or tree-flowers
    Like foam of the sea-facing tree !
No foot but the seamew's there settles
    On the spikes of thine anthers like horns,
With snow-coloured spray for thy petals,
        Black rocks for thy thorns.

Was it here, in the waste of his waters,   [*Ant.* 3.
   That the lordly north wind, when his love
On the fairest of many king's daughters
   Bore down for a spoil from above,
Chose forth of all farthest far islands
   As a haven to harbour her head,
Of all lowlands on earth and all highlands,
     His bride-worthy bed ?

Or haply, my sea-flower, he found thee   [*Str.* 4.
   Made fast as with anchors to land,
And broke, that his waves might be round thee,
   Thy fetters like rivets of sand ?
And afar by the blast of him drifted
   Thy blossom of beauty was borne,
As a lark by the heart in her lifted
     To mix with the morn ?

By what rapture of rage, by what vision   [*Ant.* 4.
   Of a heavenlier heaven than above,
Was he moved to devise thy division
   From the land as a rest for his love ?
As a nest when his wings would remeasure
   The ways where of old they would be,
As a bride-bed upbuilt for his pleasure
     By sea-rock and sea ?

For in no deeps of midmost inland May
More flowerbright flowers the hawthorn, or more
   sweet
Swells the wild gold of the earth for wandering
   feet ;
For on no northland way
Crowds the close whin-bloom closer, set like thee

With thorns about for fangs of sea-rock shown
Through blithe lips of the bitter brine to lee ;
Nor blithelier landward comes the sea-wind blown,
Nor blithelier leaps the land-wind back to sea :
Nor louder springs the living song of birds
To shame our sweetest words.
And in the narrowest of thine hollowest hold
For joy thine aspens quiver as though for cold,
And many a self-lit flower-illumined tree
Outlaughs with snowbright or with rosebright glee
The laughter of the fields whose laugh is gold.
Yea, even from depth to height,
Even thine own beauty with its own delight
Fulfils thine heart in thee an hundredfold
Beyond the larger hearts of islands bright
With less intense contraction of desire
Self-satiate, centred in its own deep fire ;
Of shores not self-enchanted and entranced
By heavenly severance from all shadow of mirth
Or mourning upon earth :
As thou, by no similitude enhanced,
By no fair foil made fairer, but alone
Fair as could be no beauty save thine own,
And wondrous as no world-beholden wonder :
Throned, with the world's most perilous sea for
    throne,
And praised from all its choral throats of thunder.

        Yet one praise hast thou, holier   [*Str.* 5.
           Than praise of theirs may be,
     To exalt thee, wert thou lowlier
           Than all that take the sea
    With shores whence waves ebb slowlier
           Than these fall off from thee :

That One, whose name gives glory,   [*Ant.* 5.
   One man whose life makes light,
One crowned and throned in story
   Above all empire's height,
Came, where thy straits run hoary,
   To hold thee fast in sight ;

With hallowing eyes to hold thee,   [*Str.* 6.
   With rapturous heart to read,
To encompass and enfold thee
   With love whence all men feed,
To brighten and behold thee,
   Who is mightiest of man's seed :

More strong than strong disaster,   [*Ant.* 6.
   For fate and fear too strong ;
Earth's friend, whose eyes look past her,
   Whose hands would purge of wrong ;
Our lord, our light, our master,
   Whose word sums up all song.

Be it April or September   [*Str.* 7.
   That plays his perfect part,
Burn June or blow December,
   Thou canst not in thine heart
But rapturously remember,
   All heavenlike as thou art,

Whose footfall made thee fairer,   [*Ant.* 7.
   Whose passage more divine,
Whose hand, our thunder-bearer,
   Held fire that bade thee shine
With subtler glory and rarer
   Than thrills the sun's own shrine.

Who knows how then his godlike banished gaze
Turned haply from its goal of natural days
And homeward hunger for the clear French clime,
Toward English earth, whereunder now the Accursed
Rots, in the hate of all men's hearts inhearsed,
A carrion ranker to the sense of time
For that sepulchral gift of stone and lime
By royal grace laid on it, less of weight
Than the load laid by fate,
Fate, misbegotten child of his own crime,
Son of as foul a bastard-bearing birth
As even his own on earth ;
Less heavy than the load of cursing piled
By loyal grace of all souls undefiled
On one man's head, whose reeking soul made rotten
The loathed live corpse on earth once misbegotten?
But when our Master's homeless feet were here
France yet was foul with joy more foul than fear,
And slavery chosen, more vile by choice of chance
Than dull damnation of inheritance
From Russian year to year
Alas fair mother of men, alas my France,
What ailed thee so to fall, that wert so dear
For all men's sake to all men, in such trance,
Plague-stricken?   Had the very Gods, that saw
Thy glory lighten on us for a law,
Thy gospel go before us for a guide,
Had these waxed envious of our love and awe,
Or was it less their envy than thy pride
That bared thy breast for the obscene vulture-claw,
High priestess, by whose mouth Love prophesied
That fate should yet mean freedom?   Howsoever,
That hour, the helper of men's hearts, we praise,
Which blots out of man's book of after days
The name above all names abhorred for ever.

So glimmers the gloom into glory, the glory recoils
    into gloom,
That the eye of the sun could not kindle, the lip not
    of Love could relume.
So darkens reverted the cup that the kiss of her
    mouth set on fire :
So blackens a brand in his eyeshot asmoulder awhile
    from the pyre.
For the beam from beneath and without it refrangent
    again from the wave
Strikes up through the portal a ghostly reverse on
    the dome of the cave,
On the depth of the dome ever darkling and dim to
    the crown of its arc :
That the sun-coloured tapestry, sunless for ever, may
    soften the dark.
But within through the side-seen archway a glimmer
    again from the right
Is the seal of the sea's tide set on the mouth of the
    mystery of night.
And the seal on the seventh day breaks but a little,
    that man by its mean
May behold what the sun hath not looked on, the
    stars of the night have not seen.

Even like that hollow-bosomed rose, inverse
And infinite, the heaven of thy vast verse,
Our Master, over all our souls impends,
Imminent ; we, with heart-enkindled eyes
Upwondering, search the music-moulded skies
Sphere by sweet sphere, concordant as it blends
Light of bright sound, sound of clear light, in
    one,
As all the stars found utterance through the sun.

And all that heaven is like a rose in bloom,
Flower-coloured, where its own sun's fires illume
As from one central and imperious heart
The whole sky's every part :
But lightening still and darkling downward, lo
The light and darkness of it,
The leaping of the lamping levin afar
Between the full moon and the sunset star,
The war-song of the sounding skies aglow,
That have the herald thunder for their prophet :
From nortn to soutr the lyric lights that leap,
The tragic sundawns reddening east and west
As with bright blood from one Promethean breast,
The peace of noon that strikes the sea to sleep,
The wail over the world of all that weep,
The peace of night when death brings life on rest.

Goddess who gatherest all the herded waves
Into thy great sweet pastureless green fold,
Even for our love of old,
I pray thee by thy power that slays and saves,
Take thou my song of this thy flower to keep
Who hast my heart in hold ;
And from thine high place of thy garden-steep,
Where one sheer terrace oversees thy deep
From the utmost rock-reared height
Down even to thy dear depths of night and light,
Take my song's salutation ; and on me
Breathe back the benediction of thy sea.

Between two seas the sea-bird's wing makes halt,
  Wind-weary; while with lifting head he waits
  For breath to reinspire him from the gates
That open still toward sunrise on the vault
High-domed of morning, and in flight's default
  With spreading sense of spirit anticipates
  What new sea now may lure beyond the straits
His wings exulting that her winds exalt
And fill them full as sails to seaward spread,
  Fulfilled with fair speed's promise.   Pass, my song,
Forth to the haven of thy desire and dread,
  The presence of our lord, long loved and long
Far off above beholden, who to thee
Was as light kindling all a windy sea.

BIRTHDAY ODE

FOR THE ANNIVERSARY FESTIVAL OF VICTOR HUGO,
FEBRUARY 26, 1880

SPRING, born in heaven ere many a springtime
    flown,   [*Strophe* 1.
Dead spring that sawest on earth
A babe of deathless birth,
A flower of rosier flowerage than thine own,
A glory of goodlier godhead ; even this day,
That floods the mist of February with May,
And strikes death dead with sunlight, and the breath
Whereby the deadly doers are done to death,
They that in day's despite
Would crown the imperial night,   10
And in deep hate of insubmissive spring
Rethrone the royal winter for a king,
This day that casts the days of darkness down
Low as a broken crown,
We call thee from the gulf of deeds and days,
Deathless and dead, to hear us whom we praise.

A light of many lights about thine head, [*Antistrophe* 1.
Lights manifold and one,
Stars molten in a sun,
A sun of divers beams incorporated,   20

Compact of confluent aureoles, each more fair
Than man, save only at highest of man, may wear,
So didst thou rise, when this our grey-grown age
Had trod two paces of his pilgrimage,
Two paces through the gloom
From his fierce father's tomb,
Led by cross lights of lightnings, and the flame
That burned in darkness round one darkling name ;
So didst thou rise, nor knewest thy glory, O thou
Re-risen upon us now,   30
The glory given thee for a grace to give,
And take the praise of all men's hearts that live.

   First in the dewy ray   [*Epode* 1.
   Ere dawn be slain of day
The fresh crowned lilies of discrowned kings'
   prime
   Sprang splendid as of old
   With moonlight-coloured gold
And rays refract from the oldworld heaven of
   time ;
   Pale with proud light of stars decreased 39
In westward wane reluctant from the conquering east.

But even between their golden olden bloom [*Str.* 2.
Strange flowers of wildwood glory,
With frost and moonshine hoary,
Thrust up the new growths of their green-leaved
  gloom,
Red buds of ballad blossom, where the dew
Blushed as with bloodlike passion, and its hue
Was as the life and love of hearts on flame,
And fire from forth of each live chalice came :
Young sprays of elder song,
Stem straight and petal strong,   50

Bright foliage with dark frondage overlaid,
And light the lovelier for its lordlier shade ;
And morn and even made loud in woodland lone
With cheer of clarions blown,
And through the tournay's clash and clarion's cheer
Laugh to laugh echoing, tear washed off by tear.

Then eastward far past northland lea and lawn
Beneath a heavier light   [*Ant. 2.*
Of stormier day and night
Began the music of the heaven of dawn ;   60
Bright sound of battle along the Grecian waves,
Loud light of thunder above the Median graves,
New strife, new song on Æschylean seas,
Canaris risen above Themistocles ;
Old glory of warrior ghosts
Shed fresh on filial hosts,
With dewfall redder than the dews of day,
And earth-born lightnings out of bloodbright spray ;
Then through the flushed grey gloom on shadowy
          sheaves
Low flights of falling leaves ;   70
And choirs of birds transfiguring as they throng
All the world's twilight and the soul's to song.

Voices more dimly deep   [*Ep. 2.*
Than the inmost heart of sleep,
And tenderer than the rose-mouthed morning's
          lips ;
And midmost of them heard
The viewless water's word,
The sea's breath in the wind's wing and the ship's,
That bids one swell and sound and smite   79
And rend that other in sunder as with fangs by night.

But ah ! the glory of shadow and mingling ray, [*Str.* 3.
The story of morn and even
Whose tale was writ in heaven
And had for scroll the night, for scribe the day !
For scribe the prophet of the morning, far
Exalted over twilight and her star ;
For scroll beneath his Apollonian hand
The dim twin wastes of sea and glimmering land.
Hark, on the hill-wind, clear
For all men's hearts to hear   90
Sound like a stream at nightfall from the steep
That all time's depths might answer, deep to deep,
With trumpet-measures of triumphal wail
From windy vale to vale,
The crying of one for love that strayed and sinned
Whose brain took madness of the mountain wind.

Between the birds of brighter and duskier wing, [*Ant.* 3.
What mightier-moulded forms
Girt with red clouds and storms
Mix their strong hearts with theirs that soar and
      sing ?   100
Before the storm-blast blown of death's dark horn
The marriage moonlight withers, that the morn
For two made one may find three made by death
One ruin at the blasting of its breath :
Clothed with heart's flame renewed
And strange new maidenhood,
Faith lightens on the lips that bloomed for hire
Pure as the lightning of love's first-born fire :
Wide-eyed and patient ever, till the curse
Find where to fall and pierce,   110
Keen expiation whets with edge more dread
A father's wrong to smite a father's head.

Borgia, supreme from birth   [*Ep.* 3.
As loveliest born on earth
Since earth bore ever women that were fair ;
Scarce known of her own house
If daughter or sister or spouse ;
Who holds men's hearts yet helpless with her
hair ;
The direst of divine things made,
Bows down her amorous aureole half suffused with
shade.   120

As red the fire-scathed royal northland bloom, [*Str.* 4.
That left our story a name
Dyed through with blood and flame
Ere her life shrivelled from a fierier doom
Than theirs her priests bade pass from earth in fire
To slake the thirst of God their Lord's desire :
As keen the blast of love-enkindled fate
That burst the Paduan tyrant's guarded gate :
As sad the softer moan
Made one with music's own   130
For one whose feet made music as they fell
On ways by loveless love made hot from hell :
But higher than these and all the song thereof
The perfect heart of love,
The heart by fraud and hate once crucified,
That, dying, gave thanks, and in thanksgiving died.

Above the windy walls that rule the Rhine [*Ant.* 4.
A noise of eagles' wings
And wintry war-time rings,
With roar of ravage trampling corn and vine   140
And storm of wrathful wassail dashed with song,
And under these the watch of wreakless wrong,

With fire of eyes anhungered ; and above
These, the light of the stricken eyes of love,
The faint sweet eyes that follow
The wind-outwinging swallow,
And face athirst with young wan yearning mouth
Turned after toward the unseen all-golden south,
Hopeless to see the birds back ere life wane,
Or the leaves born again ;   150
And still the might and music mastering fate
Of life more strong than death and love than hate.

In spectral strength biform   [*Ep.* 4.
Stand the twin sons of storm
Transfigured by transmission of one hand
That gives the new-born time
Their semblance more sublime
Than once it lightened over each man's land ;
There Freedom's winged and wide-mouthed
hound,   159
And here our high Dictator, in his son discrowned.

What strong-limbed shapes of kindred throng round
these   [*Str.* 5.
Before, between, behind,
Sons born of one man's mind,
Fed at his hands and fostered round his knees ?
Fear takes the spirit in thraldom at his nod,
And pity makes it as the spirit of God,
As his own soul that from her throne above
Sheds on all souls of men her showers of love,
On all earth's evil and pain
Pours mercy forth as rain   170
And comfort as the dewfall on dry land ;
And feeds with pity from a faultless hand

All by their own fault stricken, all cast out
By all men's scorn or doubt,
Or with their own hands wounded, or by fate
Brought into bondage of men's fear or hate.

In violence of strange visions north and south
Confronted, east and west,   [*Ant.* 5.
With frozen or fiery breast,
Eyes fixed or fevered, pale or bloodred mouth, 180
Kept watch about his dawn-enkindled dreams ;
But ere high noon a light of nearer beams
Made his young heaven of manhood more benign,
And love made soft his lips with spiritual wine,
And left them fired, and fed
With sacramental bread,
And sweet with honey of tenderer words than tears
To feed men's hopes and fortify men's fears,
And strong to silence with benignant breath
The lips that doom to death,   190
And swift with speech like fire in fiery lands
To melt the steel's edge in the headsman's hands.

Higher than they rose of old,   [*Ep.* 5.
New builded now, behold,
The live great likeness of Our Lady's towers ;
And round them like a dove
Wounded, and sick with love,
One fair ghost moving, crowned with fateful
flowers,
Watched yet with eyes of bloodred lust   199
And eyes of love's heart broken and unbroken trust.

But sadder always under shadowier skies,   [*Str.* 6.
More pale and sad and clear

Waxed always, drawn more near,
The face of Duty lit with Love's own eyes;
Till the awful hands that culled in rosier hours
From fairy-footed fields of wild old flowers
And sorcerous woods of Rhineland, green and hoary,
Young children's chaplets of enchanted story,
The great kind hands that showed
Exile its homeward road,   210
And, as man's helper made his foeman God,
Of pity and mercy wrought themselves a rod,
And opened for Napoleon's wandering kin
France, and bade enter in,
And threw for all the doors of refuge wide,
Took to them lightning in the thunder-tide.

For storm on earth above had risen from under,
Out of the hollow of hell,   [*Ant.* 6.
Such storm as never fell
From darkest deeps of heaven distract with thunder;
A cloud of cursing, past all shape of thought,   221
More foul than foulest dreams, and overfraught
With all obscene things and obscure of birth
That ever made infection of man's earth;
Having all hell for cloak
Wrapped round it as a smoke
And in its womb such offspring so defiled
As earth bare never for her loathliest child,
Rose, brooded, reddened, broke, and with its breath
Put France to poisonous death;   230
Yea, far as heaven's red labouring eye could glance,
France was not, save in men cast forth of France.

Then,—while the plague-sore grew   [*Ep.* 6.
Two darkling decades through,
And rankled in the festering flesh of time,—

Where darkness binds and frees
   The wildest of wild seas
In fierce mutations of the unslumbering clime,
  There, sleepless too, o'er shuddering wrong
One hand appointed shook the reddening scourge of
   song.   240

And through the lightnings of the apparent word
Dividing shame's dense night   [*Str.* 7.
Sounds lovelier than the light
And light more sweet than song from night's own
   bird
Mixed each their hearts with other, till the gloom
Was glorious as with all the stars in bloom,
Sonorous as with all the spheres in chime
Heard far through flowering heaven : the sea,
   sublime
Once only with its own
Old winds' and waters' tone,   250
Sad only or glad with its own glory, and crowned
With its own light, and thrilled with its own
   sound,
Learnt now their song, more sweet than heaven's
   may be,
Who pass away by sea ;
The song that takes of old love's land farewell,
With pulse of plangent water like a knell.

And louder ever and louder and yet more loud
Till night be shamed of morn   [*Ant.* 7.
Rings the Black Huntsman's horn
Through darkening deeps beneath the covering
   cloud,   260
Till all the wild beasts of the darkness hear ;
Till the Czar quake, till Austria cower for fear,

Till the king breathe not, till the priest wax pale,
Till spies and slayers on seats of judgment quail,
Till mitre and cowl bow down
And crumble as a crown,
Till Cæsar driven to lair and hounded Pope
Reel breathless and drop heartless out of hope,
And one the uncleanest kinless beast of all
Lower than his fortune fall ;   270
The wolfish waif of casual empire, born
To turn all hate and horror cold with scorn.

Yea, even at night's full noon   [*Ep.* 7.
Light's birth-song brake in tune,
Spake, witnessing that with us one must be,
God ; naming so by name
That priests have brought to shame
The strength whose scourge sounds on the
smitten sea ;
The mystery manifold of might
Which bids the wind give back to night the things of
night.   280

Even God, the unknown of all time ; force or
thought,   [*Str.* 8.
Nature or fate or will,
Clothed round with good and ill,
Veiled and revealed of all things and of nought,
Hooded and helmed with mystery, girt and shod
With light and darkness, unapparent God.
Him the high prophet o'er his wild work bent
Found indivisible ever and immanent
At hidden heart of truth,
In forms of age and youth   290
Transformed and transient ever ; masked and
crowned,

From all bonds loosened and with all bonds bound,
Diverse and one with all things ; love and hate,
Earth, and the starry state
Of heaven immeasurable, and years that flee
As clouds and winds and rays across the sea.

But higher than stars and deeper than the waves
Of day and night and morrow   [*Ant.* 8.
That roll for all time, sorrow
Keeps ageless watch over perpetual graves.   300
From dawn to morning of the soul in flower,
Through toils and dreams and visions, to that
     hour
When all the deeps were opened, and one doom
Took two sweet lives to embrace them and entomb,
The strong song plies its wing
That makes the darkness ring
And the deep light reverberate sound as deep ;
Song soft as flowers or grass more soft than sleep,
Song bright as heaven above the mounting bird,
Song like a God's tears heard   310
Falling, fulfilled of life and death and light,
And all the stars and all the shadow of night.

     Till, when its flight hath past   [*Ep.* 8.
          Time's loftiest mark and last,
     The goal where good kills evil with a kiss,
          And Darkness in God's sight
          Grows as his brother Light,
     And heaven and hell one heart whence all the
          abyss
          Throbs with love's music ; from his trance
Love waking leads it home to her who stayed in
     France.   320

But now from all the world-old winds of the air [*Str*. 9.
One blast of record rings
As from time's hidden springs
With roar of rushing wings and fires that bear
Toward north and south sonorous, east and west,
Forth of the dark wherein its records rest,
The story told of the ages, writ nor sung
By man's hand ever nor by mortal tongue
Till, godlike with desire,
One tongue of man took fire,   330
One hand laid hold upon the lightning, one
Rose up to bear time witness what the sun
Had seen, and what the moon and stars of night
Beholding lost not light :
From dawn to dusk what ways man wandering trod
Even through the twilight of the gods to God.

From dawn of man and woman twain and one [*Ant*. 9.
When the earliest dews impearled
The front of all the world
Ringed with aurorean aureole of the sun,   340
To days that saw Christ's tears and hallowing breath
Put life for love's sake in the lips of death,
And years as waves whose brine was fire, whose foam
Blood, and the ravage of Neronian Rome ;
And the eastern crescent's horn
Mightier awhile than morn ;
And knights whose lives were flights of eagles'
        wings,
And lives like snakes' lives of engendering kings ;
And all the ravin of all the swords that reap
Lives cast as sheaves on heap   350
From all the billowing harvest-fields of fight ;
And sounds of love-songs lovelier than the light.

The grim dim thrones of the east   [*Ep.* 9.
    Set for death's riotous feast
Round the bright board where darkling centuries
        wait,
    And servile slaughter, mute,
    Feeds power with fresh red fruit,
Glitter and groan with mortal food of fate ;
    And throne and cup and lamp's bright breath
Bear witness to their lord of only night and death. 360

Dead freedom by live empire lies defiled,   [*Str.* 10.
And murder at his feet
Plies lust with wine and meat,
With offering of an old man and a child,
With holy body and blood, inexpiable
Communion in the sacrament of hell,
Till, reeking from their monstrous eucharist,
The lips wax cold that murdered where they kissed,
And empire in mid feast
Fall as a slaughtered beast   370
Headless, and ease men's hungering hearts of
        fear
Lest God were none in heaven, to see nor hear,
And purge his own pollution with the flood
Poured of his black base blood
So first found healing, poisonous as it poured ;
And on the clouds the archangel cleanse his sword.

As at the word unutterable that made   [*Ant.* 10.
Of day and night division,
From vision on to vision,   379
From dream to dream, from darkness into shade,
From sunshine into sunlight, moves and lives
The steersman's eye, the helming hand that gives

Life to the wheels and wings that whirl along
The immeasurable impulse of the sphere of song
Through all the eternal years,
Beyond all stars and spheres,
Beyond the washing of the waves of time,
Beyond all heights where no thought else may climb,
Beyond the darkling dust of suns that were,
Past height and depth of air ;   390
And in the abyss whence all things move that are
Finds only living Love, the sovereign star.

Nor less the weight and worth   [*Ep.* 10.
Found even of love on earth
To wash all stain of tears and sins away,
On dying lips alit
That living knew not it,
In the winged shape of song with death to play :
To warm young children with its wings,
And try with fire the heart elect for godlike things. 400

For all worst wants of all most miserable   [*Str.* 11.
With divine hands to deal
All balms and herbs that heal,
Among all woes whereunder poor men dwell
Our Master sent his servant Love, to be
On earth his witness ; but the strange deep sea,
Mother of life and death inextricate,
What work should Love do there, to war with fate ?
Yet there must Love too keep
At heart of the eyeless deep   410
Watch, and wage war wide-eyed with all its
    wonders,
Lower than the lightnings of its waves, and
    thunders

Of seas less monstrous than the births they bred ;
Keep high there heart and head,
And conquer : then for prize of all toils past
Feel the sea close them in again at last.

A day of direr doom arisen thereafter   [*Ant.* 11.
With cloud and fire in strife
Lightens and darkens life
Round one by man's hand masked with living
　　laughter,   420
A man by men bemonstered, but by love,
Watched with blind eyes as of a wakeful dove,
And wooed by lust, that in her rosy den
As fire on flesh feeds on the souls of men,
To take the intense impure
Burnt-offering of her lure,
Divine and dark and bright and naked, strange
With ravenous thirst of life reversed and change,
As though the very heaven should shrivel and swell
With hunger after hell,   430
Run mad for dear damnation, and desire
To feel its light thrilled through with stings of fire.

　　Above a windier sea,   [*Ep.* 11.
　　　The glory of Ninety-three
Fills heaven with blood-red and with rose-red
　　beams
　　　That earth beholding grows
　　　Herself one burning rose
Flagrant and fragrant with strange deeds and
　　dreams,
　　　Dreams dyed as love's own flower, and deeds
Stained as with love's own life-blood, that for love's
　　sake bleeds.   440

And deeper than all deeps of seas and skies   [*Str.* 12.
Wherein the shadows are
Called sun and moon and star
That rapt conjecture metes with mounting eyes,
Loud with strange waves and lustrous with new
        spheres,
Shines, masked at once and manifest of years,
Shakespeare, a heaven of heavenly eyes beholden ;
And forward years as backward years grow golden
With light of deeds and words
And flight of God's fleet birds,   450
Angels of wrath and love and truth and pity ;
And higher on exiled eyes their natural city
Dawns down the depths of vision, more sublime
Than all truths born of time ;
And eyes that wept above two dear sons dead
Grow saving stars to guard one hopeless head.

Bright round the brows of banished age had
        shone   [*Ant.* 12.
In vision flushed with truth
The rosy glory of youth   459
On streets and woodlands where in days long gone
Sweet love sang light and loud and deep and dear :
And far the trumpets of the dreadful year
Had pealed and wailed in darkness : last arose
The song of children, kindling as a rose
At breath of sunrise, born
Of the red flower of morn
Whose face perfumes deep heaven with odorous
        light
And thrills all through the wings of souls in flight
Close as the press of children at His knee
Whom if the high priest see,   470

Dreaming, as homeless on dark earth he trod,
The lips that praise him shall not know for God.

      O sovereign spirit, above   [*Ep.* 12.
         All offering but man's love,
   All praise and prayer and incense undefiled !
       The one thing stronger found
       Than towers with iron bound ;
  The one thing lovelier than a little child,
    And deeper than the seas are deep,   479
And tenderer than such tears of love as angels weep.

Dante, the seer of all things evil and good, [*Str.* 13.
Beheld two ladies, Beauty
And high life-hallowing Duty,
That strove for sway upon his mind and mood
And held him in alternating accord
Fast bound at feet of either : but our lord,
The seer and singer of righteousness and wrong
Who stands now master of all the keys of song,
Sees both as dewdrops run
Together in the sun,   490
For him not twain but one thing twice divine ;
Even as his speech and song are bread and wine
For all souls hungering and all hearts athirst
At best of days and worst,
And both one sacrament of Love's great giving
To feed the spirit and sense of all souls living.

The seventh day in the wind's month, ten years
     gone   [*Ant.* 13.
Since heaven-espousing earth
Gave the Republic birth,
The mightiest soul put mortal raiment on   500

That came forth singing ever in man's ears
Of all souls with us, and through all these years
Rings yet the lordliest, waxen yet more strong,
That on our souls hath shed itself in song,
Poured forth itself like rain
On souls like springing grain
That with its procreant beams and showers were fed
For living wine and sacramental bread ;
Given all itself as air gives life and light,
Utterly, as of right ;　　　　　　　　　　510
The goodliest gift our age hath given, to be
Ours, while the sun gives glory to the sea.

Our Father and Master and Lord,　　[*Ep.* 13.
Who hast thy song for sword,
For staff thy spirit, and our hearts for throne ;
As in past years of wrong,
Take now my subject song,
To no crowned head made humble but thine own ;
That on thy day of worldly birth
Gives thanks for all thou hast given past thanks of
all on earth.　　　　　　　　　　520

NOTES

v. 33. *Odes et Ballades*, 1822–1824.

   57. *Les Orientales*, 1829.

   69. *Les Feuilles d'Automne*, 1831.

   71. *Les Chants du Crépuscule*, 1835.

   73. *Les Voix Intérieures*, 1837.

   81. *Les Rayons et les Ombres*, 1840.

  101. *Hernani*, 1830.

  105. *Marion de Lorme*, 1831.

  109. *Le Roi s'amuse*, 1832.

  113. *Lucrèce Borgia*, 1833.

  121. *Marie Tudor*, 1835.

  127. *Angelo, Tyran de Padoue*, 1835.

  129. *La Esmeralda*, 1836.

  133. *Ruy Blas*, 1838.

  137. *Les Burgraves*, 1842.

  153. *Cromwell*, 1827 : *Étude sur Mirabeau*, 1834 (*Littérature et Philosophie mêlées*, 1819–1834).

  177. *Han d'Islande*, 1823. *Bug-Jargal*, 1826.

  182. *Le Dernier Jour d'un Condamné*, 1829 : *Claude Gueux*, 1834.

  193. *Notre-Dame de Paris*, 1831.

  205. *Le Rhin*, 1845.

  216. *Napoléon le Petit*, 1852. *Châtiments*, 1853. *Histoire d'un Crime*, 1877.
In this place I must take occasion to relieve my conscience from a sense of duty unfulfilled so long as I for one have not uttered my own poor private protest—worthless and weightless though it may seem, if cast as a grain into the scale of public opinion—against a projected insult at once to contemporary France and to the present only less than to past generations of Englishmen.

PRINTED BY
WILLIAM CLOWES AND SONS, LIMITED,
LONDON AND BECCLES.